Contents

Introduction

There is nothing quite like downing a pint in the snug tavern of a centuries-old colonial inn. The creaky floorboards, rough-hewn beams, and the smell of wood smoke—it is a classic New England experience.

The six-state region that is New England—Massachusetts, Vermont, New Hampshire, Maine, Rhode Island, and Connecticut—is home to some of America's oldest inns and taverns, and they are also among the most historic and storied public houses in the country.

New England can lay claim as the home of many of the patriots of the American Revolution, colonial A-listers if you will, known by every school child in America: Paul Revere, John Hancock, John Adams, and Ethan Allen. And the entire region is dotted with landmarks and historical sites that celebrate critical battles: Boston's Freedom Trail, Lexington's Minuteman National Park, Fort Griswold State Park—all part of the path to American Independence.

It is amazing to think that the first whispers of the American Revolution were discussed within the walls of many of these surviving taverns and inns. Boston's Union Oyster House, Concord's Colonial Inn, and the Equinox in Manchester, Vermont, have all seen their share of rabble-rousing hell-raisers.

New Englanders share a profound sense of pride in their role in shaping America's history. So perhaps it is not all that surprising that so many of the region's historic colonial inns and taverns have been preserved from modernity's raid.

Each of these inns and taverns has a past—and really long ones at that. Some of these buildings date back to the 1600s. You'll find them throughout the region: on the village greens of out-of-the past hamlets; down twisting lanes of farms that are far, far away; along the scenic coastline; and even in major cities including Boston, Newport, and New Haven.

Today, travelers to these inns and taverns have an opportunity to experience American hospitality as it existed during colonial times. There is nothing more tried and true than a restaurant or an inn that has been around for several hundred years.

And there really is a historic New England inn or tavern to suit every mood. Some retain the character of their illustrious past, such as the antique elegance of Newport's Francis Malbone House or the cozy comfort of New Hampshire's Hancock Inn. While others, such as Eben House, a quirky boutique inn in Provincetown, and Ordinary, a stylish vintage speakeasy-style cocktail bar in New Haven, can best be described as channeling the past, with updated interiors that accent their historic charm.

* * *

This book is meant to be a selective summary of the region's notable, best, and most distinctive colonial inns and taverns. Of course, not all colonial inns and taverns are created equal. Some are included for purely historic reasons or for their locale, some because of the individuality of their owners, and some because there is something unique about the place—often an intangible feeling that is quintessentially New England.

Altogether, colonial inns and taverns profiled here represent a unique collection of places to visit. Rounding out the book is a list of 21 of the region's tavern history museums. Often part of town historical societies, these museums delve into the local history of tavern keeping.

Menu

→ ham + vegetable breakfast burrito

→ fresh strawberry trifle

→ fresh berries + melon

→ carrot muffins

→ currant scones

Places included in this book all hold a pedigree, and almost all are older than America. For the purposes of our collection, the year 1800 makes a lot of sense; capturing inns and taverns established in the years before, during and immediately after the founding of the Republic. And because there are a lot of ways to enjoy colonial history, there is also a smattering of inns and taverns of more recent vintage that exist today in colonial-era structures.

How accurate are the dates? That depends. Tracing the founding dates for these taverns and inns across the centuries is inexact. Longevity claims are often based on legend and rumor. And business owners are not always good memory keepers. Many of these places have opened, closed, and reopened again; some burned down and were rebuilt; others have moved buildings, changed names, or become shops or private homes along the way.

It's easy to feel as if you have gone back in time when you step across the threshold of these inns and taverns. There's a sense of history, a colonial spirit, and a very definite sense of place. All of these colonial inns and taverns help to tell the region's remarkable story, keeping New England's heritage, values, and traditions alive.

History on Tap:
Inns & Taverns in New England

Colonial America (1620–1763)

From the earliest days of New England's settlement, there have been watering holes bent on liquoring up the population. The tavern in colonial America, or the "ordinary" as it was referred to in early New England, was an important part of the social, political, and travel lives of colonial citizens.

The Mayflower passengers who eventually became known as Pilgrims were the first large group of colonists to arrive in New England, landing in what is now Massachusetts, in 1620 and settling near Plymouth. When we think of the Pilgrims, we tend to think of a dour and pious lot. But forget temperance. Beer and other fermented beverages were staples from the earliest days of Plimoth Plantation. In fact, given the sanitary conditions of the times, beer and hard cider were considered safer to drink than water.

Early Americans enjoyed their alcohol, and were a resourceful people too, using whatever raw ingredients were close at hand, including corn, apples, pumpkins, and later, imported barley, to produce their fermented beverages.

By 1630 the first Puritan settlers had moved to the Boston area, then called "Shawmut" by the Native Americans and later established as the capital of Massachusetts Bay Colony. Initially brewing and drinking took place in the home, but it wasn't long before more taverns and inns were serving alcohol and food to the public. The city's first ordinary, owned by Samuel Cole, was opened as Cole's Inn in 1634. And although drinking was an acceptable part of social life in 17th-century New England, public drunkenness was not. The Puritans were not opposed to drinking in moderation. They even mandated that each town have a tavern located close to its meetinghouse so that congregants could warm up, inside and out, after Sunday morning services, before returning for afternoon worship. But they were expected to keep their decorum.

Revolutionary Period (1764–1789)

By the 1690s New England was no longer strictly Puritan, and religious theocracy was replaced by new political ideas that were leading the colony toward revolution.

By the early 1700s, the number of public houses in Boston had risen steadily. Already a major port city, Boston had dozens of taverns along the harbor front that catered to sailors, longshoremen, and shipbuilders.

Hard cider and ale were widely available, and colonial taverns would commonly brew their own. But by the 1770s, rum was the drink of choice. With more than 150 distilleries, New England was the world leader in rum production, but it came with a price. Produced from sugar cane and traded for slaves, New England's rum heritage also has a link to a dark past.

Throughout the rest of the 18th century, inns and taverns became increasingly common throughout New England. The travel and transportation modes of the time—walking, horseback, and stagecoach—necessitated the location of inns every 10 miles or so along major travel routes.

It's hard to know which came first in New England, the tavern or the inn. In colonial times, inns offered food and drink along with a few private rooms for sleeping. Taverns may have offered only food and drink, but after too many tankards a customer could usually flop down on a hard pallet in a communal room upstairs.

In rural farming and fishing communities, inns and taverns were an integral part of daily colonial life. Besides providing food and shelter for travelers, inns and taverns were places for locals to socialize and gather, places to hold assemblies and legal proceedings, to get mail or the newspaper, to transact business, to gamble and gossip, and especially in the mid-1700s, to discuss over drinks the political issues of the day. In the period leading up to the Revolutionary War and during the war itself, taverns were often used as recruiting stations and for deployment points of the local militia—and the free ale, undoubtedly, only helped the cause.

In the decades immediately after the Revolutionary War, stage travel improved dramatically. In 1772 stagecoaches rattled over long, rutted roads, and a journey from Boston to New York would routinely take a week or two. By 1785 stages were reaching New York in just three days. As New Englanders were newly mobile, more and better inns were constructed throughout the region. Stagecoach travel sustained New England's taverns through the 1830s when railroad travel and eventually the automobile changed the transportation scene forever.

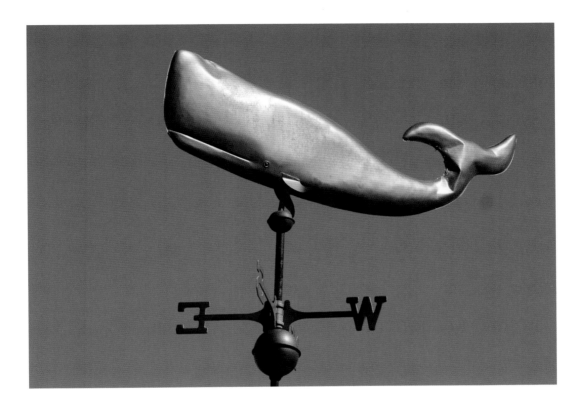

artists. Guests wake up to a continental breakfast that includes coffee, scones, cereal, juice, and fresh fruit served in the formal dining room on white Wedgewood Nantucket Basket plates.

The evening is a time to kick back. Find the stairs next to Room 10 and carefully climb (it's steep) the ladder, lift the hatch to the rooftop widow's walk, and toast the sunset. Late at night, it is also a great spot for stargazing.

Says Trich about Nantucket's popularity, "When you come to Nantucket, you actually feel that you are somewhere else, even though you are not that far from the mainland. A lot of people come here because they can immediately be gone."

9 Cliff Road • Nantucket, MA 02554 • (508) 228-9480 • clifflodgenantucket.com

Concord's Colonial Inn

CIRCA: 1716

Welcoming Travelers to a Treasured American Town

Just 15 miles northwest from downtown Boston, Revolutionary War history lies thick on the ground in Concord—from the Old North Bridge, where the Minutemen gathered to fire pot shots at the marching British Army, to Walden Pond's idyllic piney woods, to the traditional colonial village green with its steepled churches and lantern-lit town center.

The heart of Concord is Monument Square. Laid out in 1635, the street is still lined with antique structures, but today the buildings house a mix of museums, trendy boutiques, and private residences along with the venerable Concord Inn.

The Concord Inn is actually one of the oldest ongoing commercial sites in the country. The inn was originally three separate structures—the earliest of which dates from 1716. Along the way, the building has also been a doctor's office, a store, and a boarding house.

Today's Colonial Inn has just 56 rooms, but operates as a full-scale hotel with 2 restaurants and a tavern. It's a charmingly authentic New England building, which helps offset the lack of an elevator, the closets in odd places, and the doors to nowhere that are found throughout.

Visitors can choose from among 15 historic guest rooms in the main inn, 30 modern rooms in the Prescott Wing, several cottages, and a stand-alone guesthouse. The idiosyncratic rooms in the original inn have a few common dominators: wide-plank floors, decorative (non-working) fireplaces, reproduction-antique furniture, and handsome floral upholstery. Rooms in the Prescott Wing are spacious and filled with traditional, unfussy furnishings.

The inn's two on-site restaurants, Merchant's Row and Liberty, celebrate the region's agricultural roots with menus largely sourced from local farms and artisans. Here you'll find New England–centric dishes such as crab-stuffed haddock, chicken potpie, and Yankee pot roast, along with more contemporary choices such as homemade flatbreads and bacon-wrapped brussels sprout bites.

In the warmer months, there is no better place to be than the Concord Inn's spacious flag-decked front porch to people watch and enjoy a bite to eat. The lunch menu includes burgers with

cheddar cheese and New Hampshire bacon, clam chowder, and a New England chopped salad of romaine, dried cranberries, sweet potatoes, and a maple vinaigrette. In the evening it's the place to have a glass of wine and share a farmhouse board with artisan cheese and cured meats.

Famous names on the Colonial Inn's "slept here/dined here" list include Franklin Delano Roosevelt, John Wayne, Arnold Palmer, Queen Noor of Jordan, Sandra Day O'Connor, Doris Kearns Goodwin, Bruce Springsteen, and Annie Leibovitz.

"People come to the Colonial Inn because they are drawn to their American roots," says former employee Arthur Martin.

Arthur, now retired, worked as a waiter at the Colonial Inn for 17 years and is known as its resident historian. Arthur is a natural raconteur and a bit of a ham. "I would give the history spiel to the tour bus groups while running back and forth between the kitchen and dining room, making sure that the salads were ready to go," he chuckles.

The Colonial Inn, a storehouse at the time, played a significant role in the events of April 18th and 19th of 1775. It served as a munitions warehouse for colonists during the battles of Lexington and Concord, along with several other sites in Concord. The battle at Concord was forever immortalized by Concord resident Ralph Waldo Emerson's poem "The Concord Hymn" as the "shot heard round the world."

Another epic poem, Henry Wadsworth Longfellow's "Paul Revere's Ride," "One if by land and two if by sea," tells the tale of the effort to warn the colonists of the British Regular's approach to Concord. Arthur likes to remind guests that Revere never made it to Concord. "Revere was captured by the British in Lincoln. It was Doctor Samuel Prescott who delivered the message to Concord. The inn's Prescott Wing is named after Doc. He was a local boy, and he evaded the British patrols because knew the back roads."

In Arthur's version of the Battle of Concord the Concord, Inn always has center stage; "If you sit in the inn's Thoreau Room and look out the window, that's where the battle ended. The battles of Lexington and Concord set it all in motion. That's why we have the flag we have flying. "

The inn has several other important historical associations as well. In 1799 the property was bought by John Thoreau, the grandfather of author and transcendentalist Henry David Thoreau. Henry David Thoreau's father, also named John, lived here for a short time in 1835. John's sisters, Henry David's aunts, were the principal occupants of the building for many years. At the time, locals referred to the house as the "Thoreau Girls' Place." The women were well known in town for

entertaining a steady stream of visitors in the front parlor, including abolitionist Frederick Douglass, and other like-minded thinkers to discuss slavery and other issues of the day.

The building has had many owners over its lifetime. By 1861 the property became a bona fide inn and was named the Thoreau House after Henry David's aunts. In 1900 the property was renamed Concord's Colonial Inn. Today, the Colonial Inn is still a family business, recently bought by the Harrington family, owners of Sturbridge's Publick House.

But it is Concord's Minot family, which figures prominently in the first 80 years of the building's history, that is likely the source of the inn's rumored hauntings. Of Dr. Timothy Minot, Martin says, "Back in those days, if you had a hammer, a saw, and a bottle of rum, you were a surgeon."

During the Battle of Concord, Minot opened his home to the injured. The inn's second floor was used as a field hospital for the wounded colonials. The inn's Room 24 is located here today and is known to have particularly high levels of paranormal activity.

Over the years guests have reported seeing apparitions of colonial soldiers, hearing unexplained footsteps on the stairs, and knockings on the doors. Arthur doesn't doubt that something is going on at the inn.

"There isn't a day that goes by that the inn doesn't do a birthday, anniversary, a bridal shower, wedding, baby shower, a promotion or retirement party," he explains. "These folks take life-long memories of the Colonial Inn with them. With that, they leave behind a bit of energy, or spirit, if you will. My explanation of the hauntings is that Concord's Colonial Inn is loaded with more than 300 years of spirit."

48 Monument Square • Concord, MA 01742 • (987) 369-9200 • concordscolonialinn.com

Eben House
CIRCA: 1776

A Stylish Blend of the Very Old and the Very New

Bound by the Atlantic on three sides and located at the fingertip of the outstretched arm that is Cape Cod sits tiny Provincetown. While locals sometimes refer to Provincetown as the last city in America, it was actually the first place in the New World where the *Mayflower* Pilgrims made landfall before going on to Plymouth.

Today Provincetown (popularly called P-town) is a dizzying blend of a seaside beach resort, avant-garde artist colony, and Portuguese fishing village. It's a gorgeous, fascinating little place.

Bustling Commercial Street, which runs parallel along the harbor is the town's main drag, and more than just geographically. Especially in high summer, Commercial Street, with its boutiques, restaurants, bars, and art galleries is the place to see and be seen—an endless, colorful parade of humanity. Provincetown is a place that likes to have a good time.

Provincetown's isolation has a long history of attracting outcasts. Among its early colonial settlers were seafaring folk from England and Nova Scotia. Whaling and fishing were the heart of the local economy for much of the 18th century. There were pirates too.

By the early 20th century, the stark beauty of the sand dunes, the vastness of the open ocean, and the area's breathtaking silvery light caught the attention of artists, writers, and intellectuals as well as a nascent gay community. Provincetown is still known for its longstanding embrace of diversity with tolerance and a progressive attitude—everyone is welcome and accepted here.

Located a block from the raucous revelry of Commercial Street, Eben House debuted as a boutique bed-and-breakfast in 2015. From its white clapboard exterior to its flower bedecked courtyard, Eben House has New England charm written all over it. But there is no dingy floral wallpaper or dusty decor here. Eben House is very much a traditional inn with a modern twist.

The hotel is a collaboration between David Bowd and Kevin O'Shea, partners in business and in life. Together, they own Salt Hotels, a portfolio of hotel properties that includes not only Eben House, but also Provincetown's Salt House Inn.

Menu

→ ham + vegetable breakfast burrito

→ fresh strawberry trifle

→ fresh berries + melon

→ carrot muffins

→ currant scones

Bowd, originally from England, has worked in the hotel business for more than 30 years, eventually running hotels and then working at the corporate level for Andre Balazs Properties.

"I was getting further and further away from the guests. And I missed it," he explains. Kevin's background is equally impressive. He has a degree in interior design from the Rhode Island School of Design (RISD), worked in corporate design for Starwood and Morgan's Hotel Group, and has his own interior design studio.

Together David and Kevin meticulously restored the collection of three buildings that makes up the inn and in the process have created a new narrative for the property. Named Eben House as an homage to the building's first owner, Captain Eben Snow, the house was built in 1776 in the grand Federal style. A true "Captain's House," it was the first brick house in Provincetown, built with bricks that were once used as ballast on Snow's ships.

By the early 1800s the house was owned by David Fairbanks, a founder of Provincetown's Union Wharf Bank that would later become today's Seaman's Bank. Kevin says, "I've been told that some of the bank's earliest transactions took place in our living room."

In 1976, the 200th anniversary of the nation's birth, the house became the David Fairbanks House, a museum dedicated to early American art and furniture. By the early 1980s the house was converted to a guesthouse and renamed the Fairbanks Inn.

When the Fairbanks Inn became available in 2013, David and Kevin saw the opportunity to grow their boutique hotel brand. Kevin explains that from a design aesthetic his philosophy is to combine a bed-and-breakfast with the luxury of an urban boutique hotel. "I want people to have an authentic experience, to feel a connection to the building and to Cape Cod."

It is a captivating design. The decor for each spacious and airy guestroom is unique, yet it all comes together with a shared design theme—a modern take on the traditional with mixed textures and a palette of muted grays, crisp whites, and blues. Kevin had fun playing with some of the design elements. Some of the rooms have a convex mirror over the bed; it harkens back to the mirrors popular in wealthy Federal-era homes—which today just happen to make for great selfies.

"Kevin's design is very much about adding to the traditional nature and feeling of the inn," says David. These are rooms to linger in with custom mattresses, high-count linens, fresh flowers, and a really great shower experience.

And although it is an antique building, Eben House provides the modern technology that guests have come to expect, including flat-screen TVs, complimentary Wi-Fi, and loads of plugs for charging cell phones and laptops.

But the inn's signature design element is its main corridor art gallery. David and Kevin commissioned local artist Michael Kredler to create primitive portraits of a fictitious 18th-century-era family for Captain Eben. Each portrait is just a little wicked. The Captain himself sports a chandelier earring, another gentleman wears his wife's bonnet, while a rather dour woman holds a copy of the *Kama Sutra*. A blown-up Giclee on canvas version of one of the corridor portraits adds to the personality of each guest room.

At Eben House, guests feel not only pampered but that they have truly gotten away. A gourmet breakfast is served in the inn's classic light-filled conservatory and features updated breakfast classics such as a chicken sausage frittata, vanilla waffle strawberry trifle, carrot muffins, and yogurt parfaits. Guests can also choose to have breakfast in bed.

Beyond the private sanctuary of the guest rooms, there is a garden patio terrace and a sun deck, both of which provide super spots for curling up with a good book or soaking up some rays.

Innkeeping is an art—and David and Kevin share a contagious passion for Provincetown and providing personalized service for their guests. Cleaning teams are scheduled around guests' arrival times so that guests can check-in without waiting. Guests are provided a map of the guys' curated recommendations of the best local places to eat, drink, and shop. "We really want our guests to have an enjoyable visit. As much as the map is about where to go, it's about where not to go. Don't stray off the map," jokes David. "We love entertaining and our hotel business is an extension of that."

90 Bradford Street • Provincetown, MA 02657 • (508) 487-0386 • ebenhouse.com

Kelley House

ESTABLISHED: 1742

A Colonial Inn Now a Resort Hotel

Martha's Vineyard, located just off the southern coast of Massachusetts, may be the ultimate New England weekend escape. A short ferry ride through salt spray and the chop of Nantucket Sound brings the island into view with its multimillion-dollar, weathered-shingled houses; bustling historic villages; and small flotilla of boats bobbing in the harbor. Arriving at the Vineyard is forever captivating.

Known as the summer playground of celebrities and presidents—Lady Gaga, David Letterman, and Stephen King have homes here and Presidents Clinton and Obama have been frequent visitors—the Vineyard is spectacular at every turn. From its broad, sandy beaches and sea-gouged Aquinnah cliffs to its six villages full of boutiques, artist studios, and farm-to-table restaurants, the island truly is a desirable destination. With all the modern amenities, it's easy to forget that the island also has a rich colonial heritage. For years, the Vineyard has attracted generations of ordinary folks, including fisherman and farmers—and both groups flourish on the Vineyard still.

The history of Edgartown's Kelley House dates to the town's earliest settlement. Located on the eastern side of the island, the town used to be called Great Harbor and before that, on the earliest deed documents from the 1730s, it was simply called "Old Town."

The sprawling white clapboard Kelley House makes the rest of Edgartown's historic buildings, most of which are elegant, 19th-century, Greek Revival, whaling captain homes, look new.

Nis Kildegaard is a reference librarian at the Edgartown Library and the former news editor of the *Vineyard Gazette*. Nis speaks like a newspaperman, old school, of course. "The headline of this place is that it is the oldest, nearly continuously operating business on Martha's Vineyard."

The Kelley House's location, just a stone's throw from Edgartown Harbor, couldn't be better. In the 1800s ships from all over the world docked in this picture-perfect sheltered harbor.

The earliest documents referencing an inn on this site date to 1742. It was a public house called "The Tavern" and was owned by John Harper, a sea captain with a colorful past.

"Harper was born and raised in Nantucket, and suddenly he disappears from the Nantucket records and appears here in Martha's Vineyard," explains Nis. The story goes that as a young man Harper was convicted of stealing a boat, lashed in the town square, and sentenced to indentured servitude to a local mariner for his crime. Apparently Harper learned his lesson well, eventually becoming a sea captain himself, and made his fortune in the whaling business. Harper and his wife Hannah had nine children—all girls. Their daughter Bathsheba married Lemuel Kelley, and together they purchased the inn in 1762.

Says Nis, "That was the beginning of the Kelley family's association with the house. There were 20 years when it was owned by the sea captain, and from 1762 up until the 1960s the inn was in the Kelley family."

During the height of the whaling industry, Edgartown was the Vineyard's wealthiest town. After the Civil War, with whaling in decline, tourism became Edgartown's (and the Vineyard's) principal industry.

Today the Kelley House is one of the island's best-known resort hotels. But the early role of the Kelley House was that of a working inn, the idea being that there had to be a place on the island in which visiting merchants and businesspeople could stay. A great historic tidbit from Nis is that as late as the 1960s there were no locks on the guestrooms.

Says Nis, "One of the traditions of the Kelley House was that it stayed open during the shoulder season of spring and fall because that's when the Duke County Superior Court would hold its sessions. The judges, attorneys, and journalists who would come to cover the stories would stay here."

According to Nis, the turning point in Martha's Vineyard's most recent history was the Kennedy accident on Chappaquiddick in 1969. The tiny island just 500 feet off the east coast of Martha's Vineyard was the scene of a car crash by US Senator Ted Kennedy that killed his passenger Mary Jo Kopechne and ultimately would detrimentally affect his presidential aspirations. "It's still part of the community memory as a time when the world came to Martha's Vineyard," said Nis. "It wasn't the same here after that."

Edgartown's streetscape has a decidedly old-world, upscale feel, and today's Kelley House fits right in. Throughout more than 300 years of innkeeping, there have been many renovations and

several additions to the property. The inn seamlessly blends the old with the new, keeping the integrity of the historic structure and updating the interior with modern amenities.

The inn's greatest recent enhancement may just be the reestablishment of its bar. In the 1740s, the tavern was licensed to serve "strong drink" for the convenience of the wayfarers—sailors and fisherman do need their ale. However, for much of its history, the Kelley House did not have a bar or serve alcohol to its guests in the hotel's restaurant—a remnant of the Vineyard's Methodist Revival camp meeting days of the 1830s. They now offer a solid beer menu with brews from the island (Offshore Ale) and beyond, including their own Rhode Island–brewed Newes Lager. Fickle tipplers should order the rack, a five-beer sampler, and try a few.

It's best to arrive early, however, to avoid the inevitable wait for a seat. The Kelley House doesn't take reservations. This magnificently atmospheric pub, with its dimly lit subterranean space with dark wood beams and walls of ballast bricks, is well worth the wait, though. You'll find traditional pub food such as burgers, pulled pork sandwiches, and bangers and mash. And as at any self-respecting New England coastal pub, the fish and chips are excellent. In the evening, there is live local music.

The inn has 53 rooms with configurations for nearly every type of traveler. The two-bedroom Court House suites are ideal for families, with living room and kitchenette, while the 42 Garden House rooms in the main inn offer inviting coastal elegance with light-filled spaces, marble baths, and wicker and light-wood furnishings. Some rooms have balconies and views of Edgartown Harbor. Inn-like touches include coffee and muffins in the morning and cookies and milk at bedtime.

There is a family-friendly outdoor pool. Lighthouse Beach (home of Edgartown Light) is just a short walk away—both perfect places to idle away an afternoon. Looking for more activity? Rent one of the hotel's vintage bikes and take the ferry to Chappaquiddick where you can discover Mytoi, a Japanese botanical garden.

The Kelley House has been an integral part of the Edgartown community for three centuries. "[It] was the first business on Martha's Vineyard. It's still standing, still thriving," said Nis. "These days, that's a distinction."

23 Kelley Street • Martha's Vineyard • Edgartown, MA 02539 • (800) 225-6005 • kelley-house.com

Lambert's Cove Inn

CIRCA: 1790

Martha's Vineyard Bucolic Heart

If you are a romantic, then you will love this Martha's Vineyard hideaway. Located on the hilly, eastern coast of the island, this 1790s white clapboard inn is surrounded by old-fashioned gardens and a path that leads to a lovely pergola surrounded by wisteria and roses. The nearly eight acres of property also include trees, shrubs, and vegetable gardens. The quiet sound of bird song invokes the country.

Francis Foster, an amateur horticulturist, bought the property in 1901 and lived here for decades. According to owner Scott Jones, the gardens have lots of flowers that are not indigenous to the area. And, if you gain his permission first, he'll even let you take cuttings of some of them.

In the late 1700s, this property was a working family farm. The original farmhouse was small and had just two bedrooms. After a series of additions, including a post and beam barn in 1802 and a carriage house in 1804, the property became Foster's private home and a country estate before opening its doors to guests as an inn for the first time in 1970.

Scott, along with his partner and co-owner Kell Hicklin, are both transplanted Southerners—Scott is from New Orleans, Kell from South Carolina. They were both working corporate jobs in Atlanta and looking for a change when Lambert's Cove became available in 2005.

"We had visited Martha's Vineyard a couple of times and thought it was beautiful," explains Scott. "We were ready to retire, and we didn't know what we wanted to do. We thought that this might be fun." Adds Kell laughingly, "Part of the draw was that it needed work. But it was more work than we ever imagined."

Over the years Scott and Kell have thoughtfully renovated the property, preserving the many beautiful architectural details such as the grand scale of the rooms. But they've also updated it with the modern essentials travelers need to stay connected and comfy, such as Wi-Fi, television, and air-conditioning. And guests don't need to worry about tracking beach sand through the front door—each room has a private entrance.

The main inn's formal living room and library are dramatic and have an English country feel. They are decorated with antique family furniture, photos, and cut blooms. As homage to the inn's history, the guest room closets retain the faded original wallpaper of each bedroom before Scott and Kell renovated. Each of the inn's 15 guest rooms is decorated in a tranquil palette, with high-count sheets, goose down comforters, and elegant baths. The rooms have a cozy, romantic feel that will make you want to keep the curtains drawn until noon. But don't. You will not want to miss breakfast.

Breakfast is an event at Lambert's Cove. Omelets and benedicts are the stars of the menu—with eggs from the resident chickens. Each breakfast comes with toast, fruit, juice, and coffee and is so filling that you won't have to interrupt your afternoon at Lambert's Cove Beach with lunch.

Lambert's Cove guests looking for a destination spot can take the short walk to the stunningly beautiful (and secluded) beach at Lambert's Cove, or take a short drive to Edgartown or Oak Bluffs, where there is always something going on. "We are not in town and we are off the beaten path," said Scott. "Many of our guests are not first-timers to the Vineyard. They are not here for the touristy things. They walk over to the beach and they go to the pool. They play tennis and they eat in the restaurant every night."

The inn's restaurant is a real draw for both guests and the public. The 70-seat restaurant is an intimate, candle-lit space that overlooks the pool and perennial gardens, with a menu that changes weekly—it is romance defined. Executive Chef James McDonough provides an understated fine dining experience and has developed a reputation for consistent, beautifully plated dishes, such as a salad of caramelized peaches, radicchio, and arugula with goat cheese; grilled swordfish and roasted local lobster with Israeli couscous and tomato basil broth; and pan-seared George's bank scallops with lemon saffron sauce, wilted baby spinach, and red pepper coulis. Ingredients are seasonal, thanks to the inn's own gardens and partnership with island farms. Reservations are an absolute must. Says Scott, "At the restaurant, every night is Saturday night in July and August."

Scott and Kell's vision for the inn includes returning the property to its farming roots, complete with goats and chickens. "The animals are a natural progression," insists Scott. The hen house is home to fifty chickens of six different breeds that lay gorgeous eggs. Nearby is a large pen with two adorable twin goats named Ava and Zsa Zsa. Says Kell, "Our guests from Boston and New York love the idea that they can walk a goat or collect eggs in the afternoon."

The inn is closed from mid-October to mid-May, when Scott and Kell head south for the winter. They still haven't quite become used to the snow. Says Scott, "Each year we try to do something different, something new." But with the continued development of Lambert's Cove, Scott and Kell continue to share their love of the Vineyard with their passion for good food and hospitality.

90 Manaquayak Road • West Tisbury, MA 02575 • (508) 693-2298 • lambertscoveinn.com

Longfellow's Wayside Inn

ESTABLISHED: 1716

Three Hundred Years of Hospitality
on the Boston Post Road

The Wayside Inn's history stretches back to 1716, which means it has been accommodating travelers as long as nearly any place in the United States—give or take a decade.

Just ask Steve Pickford, the current innkeeper, who is eager to show a copy of the 1716 tavern license application. Then he shows an invoice that reads: "Rum 33¾ gallons. May 23, 1769, 19 pounds, 19 shillings."

"We are one of the oldest continually operating taverns in the United States," he explains. "This is our proof, just so you know."

Located at the 29-mile marker of the upper Boston Post Road, Howe's Tavern, as it was called, began as an extension of a simple four-room home and quickly became a popular stop for horsemen and stagecoaches riding the roads between Boston and New York.

The inn's first tavern keeper, David Howe, wasn't just a tavern keeper, given his land holdings—the original homestead was 125 acres—he was mostly a farmer, as well as a miller. The Howes kept the tavern in the family for nearly 150 years.

Soon after the last Howe innkeeper, Lyman Howe, died, the inn was renamed the Red Horse Tavern. Poet Henry Wadsworth Longfellow visited in 1862, along with a group of his intellectual friends, and shortly after wrote *Tales of a Wayside Inn*. The book of poems is set at a fictional Wayside Inn and describes a gathering of friends, each of whom tells a story in the form of a poem. The book was well received. Its most famous verse, "The Landlord's Tale," better known as "Paul Revere's Ride," establishes Longfellow as the poet-storyteller of a still young America.

After the Civil War, the inn fell on hard times and was used as a boarding house for itinerant workers. But the influence of Longfellow's book was profound, and the people of Sudbury began to refer to the then derelict homestead as "Longfellow's Wayside Inn."

Relief came to the Wayside in the form of Henry Ford, the industrialist and founder of Ford Motor Company, who had a modest dream to restore the Wayside Inn to a living history museum dedicated to 17th-century Americana.

Henry Ford's foundation purchased the inn, along with 3,000 additional acres around town. "He was making a little Deerfield here," explains Steve. The Wayside Inn Boys School, a trade school for orphans, was established on the property. Ford rebuilt the gristmill and had a chapel built. He also brought the one-room 1798 Redstone Schoolhouse (said to have inspired the nursery rhyme "Mary had a Little Lamb) from the nearby town of Sterling to the property. It was actually used by the town of Sudbury from 1927 to 1951 as a grade school.

Mr. Ford gave the Wayside Inn project his personal leadership until his death in 1947. And the Ford Foundation substantially rebuilt the inn after a fire gutted it in 1955.

Today, The Wayside Inn holds a wealth of treasures for visitors with an interest in American history. It is very easy to spend the better part of a day here.

There's a section of the inn's road that is unpaved—just as it was in the colonists' day. The inn's dirt parking lot is charmingly authentic, too. The weathered fieldstone and wood gristmill with its red painted water wheel is a focal point of the Wayside Inn campus and a delight to photographers. It's been tended to by Richard Gnatowski, who is also the inn's resident historian, since 1977. If you have a moment to talk, Richard has a story to tell. For example, when Henry Ford bought the inn in 1920, there was the ruin of an old mill on the property. "By my calculations," Richard offers. "I estimate that it was built around 1727." Noted engineer John Blake Campbell built the new mill in 1929 with Ford's money. The mill was built to be a historic replica, says Richard. "My thoughts tend to be that Henry Ford had a great interest in hydroelectric power. He was a great friend of Thomas Edison."

On non-milling days Richard is on hand to explain the mill's operation to visitors, but weekends are grinding days and are really the best time to visit. This is still a working mill and it produces five to ten tons of flour and cornmeal a year, much of which is used in the inn's restaurant to make johnnycakes and Indian pudding. Visitors can also buy two-pound bags of Wayside Inn flour in the gift shop.

From 1951 to 1967, the gristmill was used by Pepperidge Farm, the bakery giant, as a production facility, producing close to 600 tons of stone-ground, whole wheat flour per year. You could say that Pepperidge Farm remembers, as the company's logo is an artist's rendition of the Wayside Inn's gristmill.

Staying at Longfellow's Wayside Inn is an opportunity to sleep in an authentic piece of Americana. The inn has 10 cozy, individually decorated guest rooms available for weary travelers. Rooms 9 and 10 date from the early 1800s and are the most requested. Both rooms are also supposedly haunted. Jerusha Howe, the spinster sister of innkeeper Lyman Howe, was known as the "belle of Sudbury," and it was said she had several suitors. Jerusha was known as a gentle and refined hostess, playing the parlor piano for inn guests and working at the inn by her brother's side until her death in 1842 at the age of 45. Guests have reported hearing the sound of footsteps and piano music at certain times in the inn as well as detecting a faint floral scent perhaps left behind by a lingering spirit?

Room 10 is the nicest room in the inn, painted in Federal blue and cream and featuring a dark wood, four-poster bed with airy side curtains and a crewelwork canopy.

The guest rooms do not have any modern intrusions such as televisions, but all include a country breakfast. Guests are welcome to explore the inn and its grounds (including the garden, grounds, and school house) at their leisure. There's also the inn's Secret Drawer Society, a tradition that began in the 1950s with guests leaving notes, letters, and small tokens—literally hundreds—in every bureau and desk drawer in every guest room of the inn. What better way to while away the evening than to read other guest's "secrets." Be sure to add your own note to the stash!

Dining at the Wayside Inn allows guests to sidestep the modern rush. Choose between the inn's fine dining room or the more casual Tap Room; each restaurant has a fireplace, and they both have the same menu. The inn's signature dish is its lobster pie, and you can always count on New England classics such as pot roast and oven-roasted turkey with stuffing and cranberry sauce to be on the menu. There are lighter, more creative options, too, such as a roasted beet salad with feta and candied pecans and Maine crab cakes with a red pepper sauce.

The inn's Old Bar is the oldest room in the inn; it's a snug room with a massive fireplace and a collection of pewter tankards that hangs from the low rafters.

Have an ale or perhaps a colonial-style cocktail. The tavern specialty is the "coow woow," a stultifying mix of two parts rum to one part ginger brandy. Huzzah!

72 Wayside Inn Road • Sudbury, MA 01776 • (978) 443-1776 • wayside.org

Old Inn on the Green

ESTABLISHED: 1760

A Historic Gourmet Inn Worth the Drive

Set back from Route 57, this clapboard Georgian style inn's pillared wide porch overlooks the New Marlborough village green. A small, rural historic district that includes a meetinghouse and an old burial ground, New Marlborough was once a crossroads community that served travelers and area residents. The inn was always the center of village life. For a time, the Old Inn on the Green was an important midway point of the Hartford to Albany stagecoach line. For more than a century, from 1806 to 1925, the inn also served as the New Marlborough Post Office.

Western Massachusetts' Berkshire Hills have attracted artists, writers, and other creative types for well over a century. Tanglewood, the summer home of the Boston Symphony Orchestra, is located here, as well as several museums, historic homes, gardens, and art galleries. The area is also home to a large cluster of boarding schools. Today, the Old Inn on the Green is a gathering place for New York and Boston weekenders, for parents visiting their children at school, as well as for local residents.

Located in the foothills of the Southern Berkshires, surrounded by serene fields, meadows, and forests, Old Inn on the Green is an ideal jumping off point for a weekend getaway. Close to both Great Barrington and Lenox with their cultural attractions and shopping districts, the Old Inn is also only a short drive to more adventures: skiing at Jiminy Peak or Butternut, hiking a section of the Appalachian Trail, or fly fishing on the Housatonic River.

"This house was built as an inn in 1760," says proprietor Peter Platt. "I don't think most of our guests appreciate the age of the building and that it has been serving meals for as long as it has." According to Peter, the layout of the inn is basically unchanged except for a back addition to the kitchen that was completed 15 years ago. Much of the hardware, the doors, and some of the windows are original as well. There are four working fireplaces in the restaurant and seven more in the inn that are all wood burning, according to Peter. "[They are] not gas, and we don't use chemical logs either," he says.

The inn was unoccupied for many years until 1980 when it was bought by Brad Wagstaff and refurbished. Peter first came to the inn as the chef, and bought the property with his wife Meredith Kennard in 2004. Meredith has the innkeeping responsibilities, Peter oversees the restaurant. "We were in the right place at the right time for us," Peter says. "We've had it for over ten years now, and we are pretty happy with the way it is."

Every room in the inn has a different look. Best described as American rustic, all have an uncluttered grace, are bright, and feature antiques and folk art pieces. The inn is actually two buildings. You can stay in the original inn—but it is the noisiest because the five guest rooms are above the dining rooms. Or you can choose from one of the six rooms in the next door 1820 Thayer House for a more hideaway feel. The grounds of the inn, which feature the lawn with its the massive maples, flower-bedecked terrace, vegetable garden, and an inviting small pool, add an air of country gentry.

The experience of staying at the inn is both warm and personal. Continental breakfast is complimentary for inn guests and includes fresh orange juice, strong french press coffee, and a freshly baked pastry basket of croissants, muffins, and scones.

The inn is inviting on its own, but by far its best amenity is its restaurant, which is simply one of the best in all of the Berkshires.

The dining room has a warm, historic feel, with its simple wainscoting, a landscape mural of hills and trees, bare wood floors, Windsor chairs, and white-linen draped tables. Candlelight is the principal source of light, but the cuisine is most definitely contemporary.

Peter is one of the area's most acclaimed chefs, and he is also on the board of directors of Berkshire Grown, the region's farm advocacy group. But this is his restaurant and he is behind the line cooking every day. "We are a farm-to-table restaurant, and we do the best that we can to support our local farmers. We use the best that the season has to offer. We change what we are cooking all the time. And so we print a new menu every day."

The ingredients are always showcased, whether in a complex dish such as glazed veal sweetbreads with yellow turnip puree, pickled beets, and foraged mushrooms, or in a simple creation of pan-seared brook trout in hazelnut butter. Desserts spotlight unusual combinations such as vanilla cheesecake with a Calimyrna fig red wine sauce or a warm gingerbread with Concord grape gelato. Peter offers several prix fixe options as well, including a mid-week three-course menu that delivers a lot of food for little expense. Wines span a worldwide spectrum of regions and grapes. Nice too that there are several half-bottles that allow for sampling without a big commitment.

As Peter says, "These days, people are used to dining well." So during Tanglewood season, reservations are a must, or you will be eating elsewhere.

Along with the restaurant and inn, Peter also owns the Southfield Store, a coffee shop and cafe located a mile down the road.

A general country store has been operating in Southfield since 1907, selling practical necessities for rural New England living. Today's Southfield Store has evolved with the area and manages to be everything to everyone. In the morning the store seemingly feeds the village, selling coffee and house-made pastries. In the afternoon there are exceptional organic deli sandwiches (try the smoked ham, comte, Dijon, and tomato on rye), savory tarts, and salads to eat in the cafe or take to create a perfect picnic for an evening of music at Tanglewood. Late week (Thursday through Sunday) and in season (June through October), the cafe offers indulgent home-style dinners such as pan-roasted salmon with soba noodles or a petite sirloin with house-made gnocchi and seasonal vegetables. It's a great meal for not a lot of money.

Together Peter and Meredith have created something of a small sanctuary of cultivated, tasteful living at The Old Inn on the Green. And because the Berkshires' back roads go on forever, why not just stay the weekend?

Old Yarmouth Inn

ESTABLISHED: 1696

An Acclaimed Restaurant That Is Also Cape Cod's Oldest Inn

The wandering white clapboard colonial house stands at a bend in the byway that is Cape Cod's Route 6A. Along this now-very-busy road, you can still get a glimpse of history in its gracious 18th- and 19th-century homes. For nearly 200 years this was the halfway point for the main stagecoach route between Plymouth and Provincetown.

Still referred to as the "Old King's Highway," Route 6A roughly follows the former Wampanoag foot trails that with time became the principal cart path that, along with a journey via packet ship, was used by the earliest settlers of the Cape to travel back and forth to Plymouth, which was the principal market town and seat of government in the region during the 17th century. Early settlers were sheep farmers, but by the 18th century, many had turned to the ocean, becoming prosperous sea captains and ship owners, mostly in Far East Trade. Many of their homes still grace the route, lending this stretch of 6A the name of "Captain's Mile." Nearly 50 sea captain homes now make up the Yarmouth Historic District. Their architectural styles and superior craftsmanship stand as testaments to the town's glory days of maritime success.

Yarmouthport, a village of Yarmouth, was founded in 1639 as one of the first communities on Cape Cod. It is located on a narrow peninsula that arcs out into the Atlantic from southeast Massachusetts. The Old Yarmouth Inn has served the area for centuries. This reads as if Yarmouthport is located on a narrow peninsula. The Cape is the narrow peninsula that arcs out into the Atlantic.

According to Sheila Fitzgerald, current owner along with husband Arpad Voros, town records relating to the 17th century were lost in a fire, so much of the inn's early history is not documented. However, it is known that the building was used as both a tavern and inn, and was owned by the stagecoach company for many years. Sheila says that during its years as a stagecoach stop, first-class guests would enter through the front door to the larger rooms that were off the main staircase.

ARE HOTEL YARMOUTHPORT MASS. 7

THIS PROPERTY HAS BEEN
PLACED ON THE

NATIONAL REGISTER
OF HISTORIC PLACES

BY THE UNITED STATES
DEPARTMENT OF THE INTERIOR

Second- and third-class guests would come in through the side door and go up the stairs behind the tavern. Sheila says, "Those rooms were practically closets; there were 14 rooms in a space that 5 rooms occupy today."

By 1830, the Sears family, among the oldest and most prominent of Cape Cod, owned and operated the Old Yarmouth Inn, then named the Sears Tavern, together with next-door inn (today the well-regarded Inn at Cape Cod) as a hotel.

The inn was converted to a restaurant in the 20th century and was owned by the Peros family from the 1970s through the 1990s.

Sheila and Arpad took over the restaurant in 1996, just in time for its 300th anniversary and are devoted to preserving the feel of the inn with its 18th-century detailing and character, which they have maintained lovingly over the years. The appeal to a lot of guests is that the restaurant was once an actual colonial inn—and still looks the part with its wide pumpkin pine wood floors and original mantle. The inn's grand nine-foot, wood-burning fireplace burns from October through April. "She gets her use," says Sheila.

Next to one of the fireplaces is a door to a stairway and hidden closet. Although it is undocumented, Sheila says the inn may have had a connection to the Underground Railroad and possibly served as a safe house for slaves. The space could have also been a hiding place for liquor during Prohibition. Perhaps it was used for both.

The inn has long been rumored to be haunted. According to Sheila, Bradford Powell, who ran the inn as a boarding house for school teachers in, late 1800s, is one of the presumed ghosts. Guest and staff descriptions of Powell are consistent: He's a short, rotund man, bald but with a fringe of curly hair, and wears a wool suit with boots and big Victorian sleeves. Says Sheila, "We've had things happen from the beginning: flying ashtrays, windows blasting out, lights flickering on and off."

But don't let old Bradford scare you away from enjoying a meal at The Old Yarmouth Inn. It is a place to enjoy serious food, but it doesn't take itself too seriously. Sheila explains, "Our food is New England cuisine with a kick. We don't just serve baked haddock. We roast the panko-breaded haddock, top it with a pair of jumbo shrimp, finish the fish with a citrus beurre blanc sauce, and serve it alongside oven-roasted potatoes and asparagus. It is a pretty, pretty dish. It's also our best seller."

The Old Yarmouth Inn's classic New England clam chowder is a wonderful indulgence with its just-creamy-enough texture and meaty pieces of clam.

The rest of the menu is traditional, but steps it up with its specials such as halibut in Thai chili coconut broth, a good number of lighter dishes, and a wide variety of salads at affordable prices.

The Old Yarmouth Inn is renowned on the Cape for its Sunday Brunch, with morning saviors such as Belgian waffles, eggs Benedict, a carving station with ham and London broil, and, of course, Bloody Marys.

The inn caters to both Cape residents and tourists who choose the inn for a celebratory meal. And Arpad has skillfully chosen the wine list for both crowds. His bottle list is lengthy and varied—but there are also nearly two dozen by-the-glass options to consider. Most important? The knowledgeable servers guide you to the perfect choice.

A huge part of the Old Yarmouth Inn's recent success is its exceptional service. Sheila and Arpad foster an atmosphere of longevity. The kitchen crew has been working together for 11 years and several of the wait staff have been with the inn for more than a decade.

But the couple also has an eye to the future. "We may be one of the oldest businesses on Cape Cod," said Sheila. "But we just installed 84 solar panels on the roof. We aren't going anywhere."

223 Route 6A • Yarmouthport, MA • (508) 362-9962 • oldyarmouthinn.com

Publick House

ESTABLISHED: 1771

All Roads Lead to Sturbridge

Sixty miles west of Boston, in the quiet south central hills of Massachusetts, Sturbridge has always been at a crossroads. For the Nipmuc and Quaboag Native American tribes of this region, this area represented the intersection of several of the most heavily traveled trails connecting east and west to the Connecticut River. Today Sturbridge's east to west traffic whizzes by to and from Springfield, Hartford, Worcester, and Boston, while tour buses clog rural Route 20 on the way to visit Old Sturbridge Village, a re-created 1830's New England farming community.

Says Publick House general manager Michael Glick, "We see it as a generational crossing too—we have many families who have been coming to the Publick House for a long time and from far away. And just as in the past, we are still a popular stop on the trek between Boston and New York."

Sturbridge was first settled in the 1640s by descendants of colonists originally from Stourbridge, England. The town itself was established in 1732 and grew on agricultural, primarily small-scale farming, and as such had a town common used primarily for the grazing of livestock and for militia training. Sturbridge Common still anchors the town. There are public concerts in the summer and ice-skating in the winter. The Publick House, where travelers have checked in for supper and a good night's sleep since 1771, moors the common.

The history of the Publick House is entwined with that of the Revolutionary War. The inn was built by Colonel Ebenezer Crafts for his wife Mehitabel and, as it would turn out, their three children. Colonel Crafts was one of Sturbridge's most prominent citizens—he helped recruit and supply the Sturbridge militia for the Continental Army. It is even rumored that the inn entertained the Marquise de Lafayette during his 1824 American tour.

Crafts knew his business and developed a reputation for keeping a very good tavern. His inn had 13 overnight rooms for travelers passing through, and, as one of the region's nicer inns, it was one of the few that had a separate ladies parlor. For diversion, customers could play cards or dice in

the gaming room. And of course there was a large tap room, the place for gossip, debate, discussion, and strong drink.

After the Crafts family, the inn's prosperity continued through several owners. But by 1850, the railroad had bypassed Sturbridge going through nearby Southbridge instead. Sturbridge's economy began a slow decline. In 1923, the property became a boarding house for women and was renamed The Elms. In the 1940s, Richard Paige saved the historic building; it was his renovation that reinvigorated the inn.

Enter the Public House today and you will be struck by the irresistible waft of cinnamon from the warm-out-of-the-oven sticky buns that are the specialty of the basement Bake Shoppe. Here, on any given morning, you may run into Bob Briere and his pals at their regular table. Bob is the president of the very active Sturbridge Historical Society, "I've been president for the past 15 years. Probably because no one else wants it," he laughs. A lifelong resident of Sturbridge, Bob has a long, personal connection to the inn—he even worked there as a bellboy for a few months in 1951 when he was just out of high school. Bob is a great storyteller. He reminisces about the big parade the town held in 1942 to celebrate the Publick House's use as a training center for the Army 366th Regiment during World War II. "I was a boy, about nine years old and I still remember it," he said. "It was the only time in its long history that the inn didn't operate as public lodging or a tavern."

Hoteliers Michael and Dorothy Harrington have owned the Publick House since 2003 and are committed stewards of historic hotel properties—they also own Concord's Colonial Inn and the Hawthorne Hotel in Salem.

The Publick House is an enduring landmark of gracious hospitality. The rambling building includes 17 cozy guest rooms that feature mahogany beds and country quilts along with modern conveniences such as cable and Wi-Fi. The inn has two adjacent properties as well. At the 20-room Chamberlain House, the rooms are more spacious and have modern furnishings. Another part of the inn's property is the family-favorite Country Lodge with its 92 motel-like rooms and an outdoor swimming pool.

The original Tap Room from the Crafts period still exists at the Publick House, complete with its six-foot, open-hearth fireplace around which guests and locals mingle, evoking another place and time. Here you'll find a menu rooted in the region's history: New England baked scrod, chicken potpie, and pot roast. More contemporary choices include house-made potato chips, smoked salmon, and warm spinach salad (an excellent lunch choice), or pan-seared chicken with rhubarb compote and herbed quinoa. The Tap Room's most popular dish is its roasted turkey dinner complete with

mashed potatoes, sausage cornbread stuffing, butternut squash, and cranberry sauce. And just like at Grandma's house, there is apple pie with vanilla ice cream for dessert.

The Public House continues as a gathering place for business and socializing in central Massachusetts, and the inn still plays a large part in the rich sense of local life in Sturbridge. Every year the inn hosts a variety of community fundraisers and other gatherings. The Sturbridge Historical Society's monthly meeting draws as many as 140 passionate attendees, although Bob acknowledges, "I think they may be coming for the dessert table that the Public House donates." That's quite possible—those Bake Shoppe sticky buns are pretty darn good.

On the Common, Route 131 • Sturbridge, MA 01566 • (508) 347-7323 • publickhouse.com

Red Lion Inn

ESTABLISHED: 1773

The Hills are Alive with Berkshire Hospitality

Thanks to Norman Rockwell, Stockbridge is the Hollywood of small-town America. Rockwell lived and worked in this western Massachusetts village in his final years, often using his Stockbridge neighbors as models as he chronicled American life in the first half of the 20th century.

The iconic Red Lion Inn has stood witness to Stockbridge life for more than two centuries and features prominently in Rockwell's tribute to his adopted hometown, his 1967 painting titled *Stockbridge Main Street at Christmas.*

Berkshire County is rural, but sophisticated at the same time, especially in the summer when the area is a cultural mecca. Tanglewood, the summer residence of the Boston Symphony Orchestra, straddles the Stockbridge and Lenox town line. Chesterwood, the country home of sculptor Daniel Chester French, and the Norman Rockwell Museum are both located on the outskirts of town. Visitors can enjoy productions of the Bard's greatest works at Shakespeare & Company and visit novelist Edith Wharton's home just a short drive away in Lenox.

The Red Lion Inn, located in the southern Berkshire Hills, was established in 1773 by Silas Bingham as a general store that soon evolved into a tavern and stagecoach stop on the once bustling road headed from Boston toward New York.

In 1787 Shays' Rebellion shocked the young nation when an armed uprising of Massachusetts farmers, led by Daniel Shays, attempted to seize the Springfield Armory. The Red Lion Inn provided a haven for Massachusetts farmers, many Revolutionary War veterans who gathered to protest the government's economic policies—including the practice of foreclosing family farms and throwing debtors into prison for delinquent taxes.

And while the inn has had many owners and names over the years, it has always (or very nearly) operated under the sign of a red lion, one of the most popular pub names in England. The inn's first crest depicted a red lion with a green tail the red lion symbolizing the British Crown and the green tail said to signify sympathy to the Revolutionary cause.

The inn's feline tales carry on to this day through Simon Treadway Gato, the inn's resident cat and mascot. Simon presides over the lobby and is allowed to wander the halls and spend extra time with willing guests. But sometimes he has other important things to do—like napping.

In the late 19th century the captains of industry took up residence in the Berkshires' rolling hills, building grand "cottages" to create a summer-in-the-country idyll.

The current inn is not original—fire destroyed the entire building in 1896. The inn was rebuilt on the site of the first structure in 1897. The new inn had four floors and a birdcage elevator. Today, this glamorous relic of the Gilded Age still requires an operator to work it. Going up? Ask at the front desk. There is also a front porch that just won't quit. One of the inn's greatest pleasures is the opportunity to while away an afternoon in a rocking chair while taking in Stockbridge's Main Street, a little slice of authentic Americana.

The Red Lion Inn has the renown of being the first Berkshire County business operated by a woman. Anna Bingham was the widow of one of the inn's original owners and ran the tavern after the death of her husband. The Widow Bingham Tavern is named in her honor. The tavern represents the inn at its most historic; the dark paneled space has just six tables and a small bar, and is a cozy space for a casual meal and a drink. Wide pine planked floors, red-and-white-checkered tablecloths, vintage photographs, and other memorabilia all add to an atmosphere of good cheer. Highlights of the small menu include the hand-carved turkey sandwich with stuffing and cranberry mayonnaise and the Angus burger with local Bayley Hazen blue cheese.

All the inn owners have been collectors. Displayed amid high shelves throughout the main dining room, the inn's antique teapot collection is a stand out. The inn's historic dining room provides the backdrop to some excellent New England–centric dishes from Executive Chef Brian Alberg. All the inn's menus are seasonal and feature local ingredients. Find well-balanced salads that feature farro, kale, and olives with feta. Entrees, such as a filet mignon with truffled risotto and braised greens or salmon with a grilled radicchio panzanella salad, are both intense and meaty.

Over the years, the Red Lion has evolved to provide landmark accommodations in the Berkshires and is a destination in and of itself. "There is a lot of tradition here. We have regulars who book for next year on their way out the door," says Brian Butterworth, director of sales. "When you are at the Red Lion, you know you are in the Berkshires. We are pretty well known here as the Berkshire place."

And while the Red Lion Inn honors the past, it still has a real sense of style. Says Brian, "We are the anti-doily people. Guests who have the money to travel to places like this expect more." And, at the Red Lion, they get it. The inn has a total of 125 guest rooms of several shapes and sizes. The main inn includes 85 rooms, each outfitted in a mix of country furniture, folk art, feather duvets, and a vase of cut flowers. The bathrooms feature white wainscoting, floral wallpaper, and thick white towels. Over the years, several homes in the neighborhood have been converted to Red Lion guesthouses. The larger units feature a private entrance, multiple bedrooms, a living room, and a kitchen, along with a more chic New England aesthetic that includes designer touches such as contemporary art pieces that add wit and whimsy.

Brian describes the current trend for hotels to have lobbies that have bars and space to relax, that are more than just a place to check in. "And of course the Red Lion Inn has been doing that forever," he said. "It's the center meeting place in town."

The inn has had its share of famous visitors, hosting five US presidents (Cleveland, McKinley, both Theodore and Franklin Delano Roosevelt, and Coolidge); writers Nathaniel Hawthorne, Henry Wadsworth Longfellow, and Thornton Wilde; as well as countless musicians, including the Kiev Chamber Orchestra, Tony Bennett, and Billy Joel. Garrison Keillor stays here regularly. He probably feels right at home.

The inn has changed hands many times over the centuries. By the 1960s the owners had limited success. Jack and Jane Fitzpatrick bought the building to house their business Country Curtains. "If the Fitzpatrick's hadn't bought the building at that point, it would have been torn down," said Brian. "Country Curtains made the Red Lion possible." Indeed, Country Curtains, one of the country's largest mail order curtain companies' flagship store, still occupies space in the inn and is a great place to shop for home décor and window treatments that range from rustic to elegant.

Today the inn is run by Jack and Jane's daughter, Nancy Fitzpatrick, and her stepdaughter, Sarah Eustis. The Fitzpatrick family owns and manages several other hotel properties in the Berkshires, most notably the Porches Inn in North Adams, a complex of 20th-century millworker's homes renovated in a hip, mid-century modern design. Brian sums it up nicely, "This is the mother ship. It's our roots. Our philosophy of hospitality comes from the Red Lion Inn."

30 Main Street • Stockbridge, MA 02162 • (413) 298-5545 • redlioninn.com

The Salem Cross Inn Restaurant & Tavern

CIRCA: 1707

Gastronomic History Is Well Served Here

Amid the rolling hills of south-central Massachusetts, the Salem Cross Inn Restaurant & Tavern sits just a few yards off busy Route 9 in West Brookfield. The rambling old farmhouse is connected to an antique post and beam barn surrounded by well-tended vegetable and herb gardens. A low fieldstone wall surrounds part of the 600 acres of open fields that is home to a working heritage breed cattle farm.

The original homestead was granted to Concord resident John White in 1707, who set out "west" to make a life for himself and his young family. Located just east of the Connecticut River, the Brookfield area was at that time the "wilderness" of Massachusetts Bay Colony. It was isolated from the other, larger English coastal settlements in Boston and Salem and prone to attack by the local Nipmuc natives.

Although the Salem Cross Inn has never been in service as a lodging establishment and has only operated as a tavern/restaurant for the past 50 years or so, the historical importance of the 300-year-old farm and the opportunity to experience a little of the spirit of colonial New England farm life is tremendous.

You couldn't ask for a better tour guide of the property than Martha Salem-Leasca, whose family now owns the property. Walk with her through the restaurant and her knowledge and passion for her family's enterprise is evident—she enjoys telling a story and is proud of her family's legacy.

Martha tells how the White family farmed this land, passing the property from father to son for seven generations. The earliest part of the original clapboard farmhouse dates from 1710, while the newer 1740 addition was substantial for its time, demonstrating both elegance and style. In the main sitting room, Martha points out the wide hand-carved wood paneling with its iron-forged square nails and the central fireplace with its built-in warming cabinet. In the dining room the

original walls are discolored—even a little dingy—but have an unmistakable iridescence. Martha explains that ground seashells were mixed in with the plaster, and this method was considered a real status symbol in a home this far inland during the colonial era.

By the 1950s the White homestead had suffered from decades of neglect, and the house and adjoining barn were put up for auction. Martha's father, Henry Salem, and his brother, Dick Salem, thought that turning the farmhouse into a restaurant would be a good family project.

After a lengthy and faithful restoration (the house is listed on the National Register of Historic Places), the Salem family opened the restaurant in 1961. "The Salem Cross Inn is really the result of the vision of my father and uncle," Martha explains. Henry originally named it the "Peregrine White House," after the first child born to the Plimoth Pilgrims in the New World, but that name was short-lived. To explain, Martha points out the small hex sign on the inn's original front door latch. It's an "X" crossed with three horizontal lines. Martha explains that hex symbols were believed to help keep away evil spirits and were part of daily life in colonial New England. The Salem Witch Trials had taken place in 1692, and the fear of witches throughout Massachusetts Bay Colony was still very real in the early 1700s.

The name *Salem* is a derivative of the Arabic word *salaam* and/or the Hebrew word *shalom*, both meaning "peace." Martha, being of Lebanese descent, says that the coincidence of the Salem surname and the Salem witchcraft-era hex sign on the door was not lost on the family, so Henry and Dick changed the restaurant's name to the Salem Cross Inn just weeks after opening. "It was meant to be," she says.

Martha runs the Salem Cross Inn restaurant and tavern with her sisters Nancy and Heather, along with their brother Bo. But when asked about her position she's quick to say, "We don't have job titles. We are a family business, and we work as a team."

And as a team, they have built The Salem Cross Inn into a popular destination for busloads of history buffs visiting nearby Old Sturbridge Village and for the hordes of shoppers who descend three times a year (May, July, and September) on the Brimfield Antique Show.

Hearty, made-from-scratch fare satisfies the hungriest of travelers. At lunch you'll find standards such as grass-fed burgers and chicken potpie. More contemporary touches sneak into the dinner menu, which features dishes such as seared duck breast served with a lavender demi-glace and a cedar plank maple salmon. You might think you are in Boston's Back Bay if not for the low-ceiling wood paneled dining rooms, the many oversized fireplaces, and the eclectic mix of colonial folk art and antique bric-a-brac scattered about.

But the Salem Cross Inn is best known for its Drover's Roasts and Fireplace Feasts. Somehow, devouring large portions of red meat roasted over an open pit just feels colonial New England. The Drover's Roast occurs twice yearly in the fields surrounding the property, on Father's Day and the second Sunday in September. It's quite a spectacle—a lavish feast featuring prime rib roasted over a fire pit, groaning boards laden with seasonal sides, along with shortcake and pies. There are horse-drawn wagon rides and some of the servers wear period clothing. And, if you listen carefully, you just might hear the sounds of fifes and drums over the hillside.

The inn's popular Fireside Feasts take place on weekends from November through April and are informal and relaxed. These lively historically inspired meals are served family style at communal tables—think of it as a cross between a dinner-party and a church supper.

Pre-dinner, guests have the opportunity to leave the modern world behind and enjoy a horse-drawn wagon or sleigh ride through the farm's woods and fields. On Fireside Feast days, the prime rib is slow-cooked over a wood fire in the Chestnut Room's massive fieldstone hearth. Martha's brother Bo is in charge of the 17th-century roasting jack and enjoys explaining the spit's mechanics and the origins of the expression "done to a turn."

The Fireside Feasts are information and fun-packed programs that use period tools and cooking techniques to offer a taste of New England's past. A mulling iron is heated in the fire's coals until it is screaming hot. It is then plunged into the metal jug that holds spiced wine. The hot iron heats the wine and creates a perfect concoction to shake off the winter chill. Guests are encouraged to help stir the cauldron of clam chowder as it cooks in the fireplace. And an 18th-century apple peeler and corer is demonstrated—making short order of the dozens of apples needed to make the evening's dessert of deep-dish apple pie.

Is the Salem Cross Inn "touristy"? Yes, it is. But the Salem family is all about bringing people together to celebrate the food and culture of early New England. The Salem Cross Inn is a wonderful place to experience a meal as well as a moment in time.

---

260 West Main Street • West Brookfield, MA 01585 • (508) 867-2345 • salemcrossinn.com

Union Oyster House

CIRCA: 1640S

Freedom Trail Pit Stop

Squeeze into one of the nine bar stools at the historic mahogany oyster bar and order a bowl of clam chowder and a dozen impeccably fresh, plump, and briny Cotuits. Chase it all down with a Sam Adams 375 Colonial Ale—a red brown ale with a hint of molasses that is brewed exclusively for the Union Oyster House. Spend some time bantering with the friendly shuckers and your new barmates. And then order another dozen.

Famished and footsore, nearly every first-time visitor to Boston eats at the Union Oyster House, if only because it is located directly on Boston's Freedom Trail—the 2.5-mile long path that passes through some of the country's most historic landmarks, including the site of the Boston Massacre and and the Paul Revere House. The Union Oyster House makes for a logical mid-journey place for a rest and a bite to eat.

And while the opportunity to learn about colonial history is the hook, the food is delicious. According to Jim Malinn, the Union Oyster House's general manager, the real appeal of the Union Oyster House is that it offers visitors the opportunity to enjoy great New England cuisine along with their experience of the Freedom Trail.

The Union Oyster House is located on the Blackstone Block, one of the oldest areas of the city. The closely packed buildings and narrow, winding street offer visitors a rare glimpse of Boston's original 17th-century street pattern. When you enter the Oyster House, with its low, slanted ceiling and wide-planked floor that is so worn in places that it is soft under your feet, you will feel as if you have stepped back in time.

The building itself, a three-and-a-half-story brick gambrel, dates from pre-Revolutionary times. Facts are hard to come by when it comes to buildings that date to the 18th century, but historical architects have determined that the original structure dates from the early to mid-1700s. By 1742 the building's first business, a fancy dress good store named Hopestill Capen's,

was established at street level. From 1771 to 1775 publisher and printer Isaiah Thomas lived and worked on the second floor of the building. His newspaper, the *Massachusetts Spy*, was among the most radical of the day. Tories referred to Thomas's print shop as the "Sedition Foundry." Today, a mural on the second floor of the Oyster House depicts the life and times of the Patriot Printer, one of the greatest untold stories of the Revolutionary War.

Later, for a few short months in 1797, the same second floor rooms served as lodgings of the exiled Louis Philippe, the future (and last) King of France.

The Union Oyster House's history as a restaurant dates to 1826, when the Atwood & Bacon Oyster House first swung open its doors to diners. Atwood & Bacon was a boisterous joint, located across the street from Faneuil Hall, famed for its long history of public orations, and just a block from the waterfront. Before Boston's landfill projects expanded, the Atlantic Ocean reached almost to the structure's foundation! The bar was favored by both politicians and sailors on leave. Atwood & Bacon had a bare bones menu, but advertised oysters in every style: raw, stewed, roasted, fried, and in chowder.

In the colonial period, oysters grew naturally and plentifully in Massachusetts's coastal estuaries. They were a reliable and favored food source for the Native Americans of the region and soon became a diet staple for the early British settlers. By the early 1800s Bostonians had a passion for the tasty mollusks and oyster houses were a ubiquitous presence in the city.

For a time outspoken Daniel Webster, the Massachusetts Senator and Secretary of State under Harrison and Fillmore, was quite the regular. Apparently Webster liked to end his day at the oyster bar, pairing tumblers of brandy with plates of a half dozen oysters—and legend says that he seldom had fewer than six plates.

Today, the Union Oyster House is co-owned by Joe Milano and his sister Mary Ann Milano Picardi, and has been since 1971. Remarkably, the Union Oyster House has always been family-owned and operated and has had only four owners in its history.

And just as the Oyster House is considerably larger than it was in the 18th century (over the years the restaurant expanded to incorporate two adjoining buildings), so too are its food offerings. Aside from oysters on the half-shell, the menu offers the usual index of Boston dishes: fried seafood, boiled lobster, Yankee pot roast, baked beans, and Boston cream pie, and they are all as good as ever.

Not sure what to order? The broiled cod with seasoned breadcrumbs is particularly outstanding. It's one of those dishes that just speaks of New England.

Of course, when your eatery has been around for almost 200 years, a few famous faces are bound to stop by. In the past, showbiz stalwarts such as Meryl Streep, Clint Eastwood, and Billy Crystal have dined here. But the Union Oyster House is still relevant—Sting, Benedict Cumberbatch, and talk show host Jimmy Fallon are some of the latest celebrity sightings. President Obama even recently ordered ten bowls of chowder "to go" before boarding Air Force One after a recent Boston visit.

But according to Jim, it's the Kennedy booth on the second floor that every diner wants to see. John F. Kennedy served in both the US House of Representatives and the US Senate before becoming President. On his weekly trips to Massachusetts, Kennedy was a Union Oyster House Sunday afternoon regular, reading the newspapers over a bowl of lobster stew. His is the restaurant's most popular booth—you can reserve it in advance (but know that your meal may be disturbed by other camera-wielding tourists).

41 Union Street • Boston, MA 02108 • (617) 227-2750 • unionoysterhouse.com

Warren Tavern

ESTABLISHED: 1780

Paul Revere and His Buds Drank Here—and You Can Too

George Washington visited in 1789. Paul Revere drank here—apparently often. "Inadvertently Washington and Revere saved the tavern. Because they had been here, they saved the building from being torn down," says John Harnett, Warren Tavern's general manager.

"Many of the founding fathers were Freemasons," explains John. "George Washington and Paul Revere both were Freemasons. Historical records from the Freemasons record the individuals that were here for the meetings. We have Masonic records that show that both Washington and Revere were at the Warren Tavern."

The Warren Tavern is the oldest tavern in Boston. Cozy, with low ceilings supported by massive hand-hewn timber posts (some salvaged at a later date from ships built at the nearby Charlestown Navy Yard), pegged wood floors, and a huge fireplace. This is where you come in Boston to get a sense of a colonial tavern as it was long ago.

The Warren Tavern is located in Boston's Charlestown neighborhood, just across from the mouth of the Charles River. This area was the site of Boston's first English settlement, established by the Puritans in 1630. For most of the 20th century, the area has been a working-class Irish enclave, known for its small-time crooks and its code of silence—and made even more notorious (and tremendously romanticized) by Ben Affleck's crime film *The Town*.

The history of the Warren Tavern dates back to 1780 when Eliaphalet Newell, a baker by trade, built the tavern and offered a room upstairs for tavern visitors to stay overnight. The sparse space would have offered a place to sleep off a night of too much drink, but not much in the way of privacy. Eliaphalet was well respected among his peers, rumored to have been one of the participants in the Boston Tea Party (identities were shrouded in secrecy for fear of reprisal), and an active member of King Solomon's Lodge, allowing the Freemasons to hold their monthly meeting at his tavern for more than 20 years.

When Eliaphalet built his tavern, he named it in honor of General Joseph Warren, the charismatic 34-year-old doctor who died from a musket ball to the head during the Battle of Bunker Hill five years earlier. Warren became the Revolution's first hero, and it has been speculated that had he survived the Revolution, he would have been one of the prominent leaders of the New Republic.

The tavern is located practically in the shadow of the Bunker Hill Monument, the last stop on Boston's Freedom Trail—the path that wends its way through the city and its 16 Revolutionary War–era sites. The 221-foot granite obelisk commemorates the first major battle of the Revolutionary War between the British and the colonists. It occurred on June 17, 1775 (a holiday still celebrated in Boston), and witnessed some of the most ferocious fighting between the British and the colonists. The colonists, led by Colonel William "whites of their eyes" Prescott, were entrenched on Charlestown's Breed's Hill (where the battle was actually fought) when the British, led by British General Thomas Gage, launched a series of assaults. By the end of the day the British captured Breed's Hill and the colonists retreated. British casualties numbered just over 1,000 while the American losses totaled 400. And although the battle was a tactical victory for the British, it came at a significant price. For the colonists it represented a moral victory and proved they could fight toe-to-toe against the mighty British Army.

The tavern, which steadily deteriorated during the 19th century and suffered damage in several fires, was scheduled for demolition in 1970, but was saved in 1972 through the efforts of the Charlestown Preservation Society, which helped developer Jim Adams step in and restore it.

Partners Tom Devlin and Patrick O'Sullivan have owned the Warren Tavern since 2006, maintaining an important piece of history for the city while providing a modern place of respite and good cheer. Being located just off the Freedom Trail, the tavern gets a good number of tourists, but it is essentially a solid neighborhood family restaurant that unites folks of all ages and backgrounds—townie, young working professionals and families with kids. The menu focus is on hearty main courses that are crowd pleasers—sirloin tips, haddock with breadcrumbs, and shepherd's pie—all priced for weeknight dining. Says John, "People love our clam chowder. We've won all kinds of awards. Our seafood comes in fresh daily. And of course we have our burgers. There's really nothing like having a burger, watching the game, and having a cold beer." On Wednesday and Thursday evenings there is live music (with no cover), a better than decent beer selection (with 16 taps), and classic American tavern fare. Dr. Warren would likely approve.

---

2 Pleasant Street • Boston, MA 02129 • (617) 241-8142 • warrentavern.com

1774 Inn

CIRCA: 1774

A Romantic Maine Bed-and-Breakfast.
Is There Any Other Kind?

Set in a Revolutionary War–era home on the tidal Kennebec River, away from Vacationland tourist crowds, this bed-and-breakfast is a world unto itself—and that's a good thing.

Phippsburg is raw and genuine mid-coast Maine, a small community of just over 2,000 year-round residents. The town is less than a one-hour drive north of Portland, and is located along a finger-shaped peninsula with 60 miles of craggy shoreline and tranquil coves flanked by sweeping swaths of salt marsh and piney woods.

It's not commonly known, but the very beginnings of colonial America can be traced to this part of Maine. Popham Colony was founded at the mouth of the Kennebec River in 1607 and was the sister settlement to Jamestown Colony in Virginia. The fledgling Popham Colony did not prosper, however, and after a little more than a year it was abandoned. For their return to England, the settlers built the *Virginia*, the first oceangoing ship constructed in the New World and the beginning of Maine's shipbuilding tradition. With its long coastline, protected coves, and abundant forests, Maine led the United States in wooden shipbuilding during the late 19th century, and continues shipbuilding to this day at nearby Bath Iron Works, the General Dynamics mega-shipyard that specializes in producing US Navy destroyers.

The 1774 Inn, also known as the McCobb-Hill-Minott House, has been a local landmark for the entirety of its more than two centuries of existence. The inn's charming owners, John Atkinson and Jackie Hogg (he's from England, she's from Ireland) "retired" in 2008, purchasing the house and converting it into an inn.

The couple lives on the property in an apartment over the barn when the inn is open during the vacation season, May through October, and spend the rest of the year, known as the "quiet season," at their home in England.

In their previous lives, John worked in public relations and Jackie worked for British Airways. As John tells it, "We have a background in people. We thought, let's buy a bed-and-breakfast and we can work it together. And we just love mid-coast Maine. It's such beautiful part of America, this. We walked in the house, saw that view of the Kennebec River, and thought, right, let's go for it."

The house was built on an impressive scale and has exquisite proportions, with large square rooms, high ceilings, and big windows typical for the well-to-do of the era. It seems, however, that the house was a little grand for what was then a frontier settlement. Built by Captain James McCobb, a successful merchant, shipbuilder, and landowner (he eventually owned much of Phippsburg), for his second wife in 1774, the handsome Georgian home was nicknamed the "Mansion in the Wilderness" by its neighbors. John laughs, "[Mrs. McCobb] was obviously a demanding lady."

A noble Linden tree, also more than 200 years old, spreads shade beneath its boughs just outside the home's original front door. Called a witches door, said to ward off evil, the top panel is styled to resemble a cross, and the lower panel forms a hex sign.

"When you think that is was all done by hand, that it has stood the test of time, how it is pretty much original as it was more than 240 years ago, it is quite incredible," says John.

In the early 1800s the home was inherited by Captain McCobb's stepson Mark Langdon Hill, a prominent politician who served as US Congressman from Massachusetts and Maine (Maine was part of Massachusetts until 1820). Somewhat surprising, though is that none of Hill's 10 children or other descendants chose to live in the house after his death. In 1853 the home was purchased by Charles Minott, a "big shipbuilder in these parts," according to John. The house stayed in the Minott family until the 1960s. Charles's granddaughter Ada Minott Haggett was the last Minott to enjoy the property. John and Jackie were fortunate to have Ada and her husband around for tea before she passed away in 2013. "She was a fascinating lady, and she knew everything about the history of the house," says John.

Staying at the 1774 Inn is all about easy elegance. Jackie was the decorator for the project, and her attention to detail is evident throughout the house. The elegant living room reveals her good taste with two cream-colored sofas that face the fireplace and stand out against the yellow and gray floral wallpapered walls.

The inn's oldest and most luxurious rooms are in the main house and named in honor of each of the previous owners: McCobb, Hill, Minott, and Haggett. But the most popular room is the "Wood Shed" room, which features a four-poster queen-size bed and french doors that open to a private veranda and water views. The Wood Shed room is one of four additional bedrooms in the

attached annex building, constructed by Charles Minott in 1870 to bunk his shipworkers.

Half the charm of a night spent here is Jackie's home-cooked gourmet feast the following morning. Served in the sunny dining room with its window seats and adjoining butler's pantry, there is always a main course breakfast entree along with juice, coffee, fruit, and granola. Among Jackie's specialties are blueberry cream cheese french toast and lobster scrambled eggs.

In nice weather, guests can relax on the outdoor patio, walk the four acres of grounds, or stake a claim to one of the Adirondack chairs on the riverbank.

Looking for a lobster roll and a lighthouse? John and Jackie will point you in the right direction. The inn is within a 15-minute drive of Popham Beach State Park, a Maine gem with a golden 3-mile stretch of sandy beach. Hungry? Stop at Spinney's for a buttered hot dog roll filled with chunks of lobster meat and enjoy it with a view of Seguin Lighthouse, especially beautiful at sunset. Other possible detours include visiting the Maine Maritime Museum in Bath or heading up the road to Bowdoin College and exploring its two excellent museums: the Bowdoin Museum of Art and the Peary–MacMillan Arctic Museum, which recounts the tales of pioneering expeditions to the North Pole by Bowdoin alums Robert E. Peary and Donald Baxter MacMillan.

"The great thing is that we are living in a piece of history," says John. "Plus the fact that this is the most amazing house to live in. We've been very lucky. We have met the most fantastic guests over the years and we have made some very good friends."

44 Parker Head Road • Phippsburg, ME 04562 • (207) 389-1774 • 1774inn.com

York Harbor Inn

CIRCA: 1637

A Historic Maine Inn with a Nautical Past

The York Harbor Inn, which sits just across the street from York Harbor Beach, offers the rare combination of colonial charm and a waterfront location.

York is located along coastal southern Maine and is one of the country's oldest oceanfront towns. The first European colony settled here in the 1640s and was originally called Agamenticus, which was the Native Abenaki name for the area. In 1652 the region was renamed York, after the town in England, and came under the jurisdiction of the Massachusetts Bay Colony. And by 1692 the small provincial colonial outpost was nearly decimated by fighting with the Indians and the French during the King William's War.

But York really came into its own during the late 1800s as a summer resort town for a new middle-class lured by the woodlands, mountains, and the steel-blue Atlantic waters crashing against the rocky cliffs. These same stunning scenes bring visitors to mid-coast Maine today.

The York Harbor Inn is owned by Garry Dominguez and his family. "When we bought the inn from the Colligans in 1980, the inn had only ten rooms and an eight-car parking lot," remembers Garry.

Today the original rambling white clapboard inn has expanded to 61 rooms, which are spread among five additional 18th- and 19th-century buildings. One of the inn's most remarkable details is its "Cabin Room," an antique structure that dates from 1637. The space serves as the inn's lobby, comfortably furnished with multiple seating areas in front of a magnificent nine-foot fieldstone fireplace. Look up at the rafters and imagine fishermen draping their sails over the beams to dry them and make repairs. Originally a fishing shack, it was located on one of the Isles of Shoals, a group of small islands just five miles off the coast, now divided between Maine and New Hampshire.

The Isles of Shoals were first discovered by English and French fisherman in the 1500s and were sporadically settled. In the early 1600s the first hardy fishing communities were established there with a station for supplying the boats and drying the catch (principally cod) for shipment to England. By 1775 the beginnings of the Revolutionary War forced the fishing community to come ashore. And in typical Yankee thrift fashion, the buildings came along as well. The settlers dismantled the structures, loaded the timber on barges, and floated them to the mainland where they were reassembled.

Several of these pre-colonial Isles of Shoals buildings still exist and are scattered throughout coastal Maine. The York Harbor Inn's sail cabin was attached to the inn's original farmhouse sometime in the 1800s, when it became the Hillcroft Inn with just a handful of rooms, a tavern, and a dining room.

York remained a small farming and fishing community until the turn of the 20th century, when the York Harbor and Beach Railroad opened the area to tourism. Vacationers discovered southern coastal Maine as a summer retreat from the overcrowded and overheated cities. These tourists boarded in the dozens of simple, oceanfront inns or in one of the larger Victorian hotels that lined York's coastal road, today's Route 1A.

For many years, in the 1930s and '40s, Mrs. Florence operated the Hillcroft Inn as a trolley stop cafe and restaurant. Most of the guesthouses were wooden structures, and many eventually burned. "This inn survived because it was a lot smaller and didn't see the activity that those other places did," Garry says.

Dining at the York Harbor Inn is a treat. Executive Chef Gerry Bonsey supervises dining in all of the inn's restaurants. Garry hired Gerry more than 30 years ago. "We both started our careers pretty much together, and we both learned the business from the bottom up."

The main dining room's most sought-after tables are upstairs in front of the large picture windows that perfectly frame an ocean view. A more casual option is the Ships Cellar Pub, a cozy, welcoming space of polished teak and mahogany (like the interior of a yacht), where local beer dominates the taps, maritime bric-a-brac crowds the walls, and live music entertains all weekend long. The bar occupies the former Hillcroft Inn horse stalls. Remembers Garry, "When we bought the property, the horse stalls were actually still here made into a crude cocktail area."

Chef Bonsey's menu features creatively prepared fresh, local seafood. All the lobster, scallops, and oysters are hauled fresh from the waters of York Harbor each day. Favorites include mussels Provençal, baked stuffed lobster in a brandy sauce, or even a juicy, perfectly cooked burger. But the inn is equally renowned for its creamy seafood chowder and its lobster stuffed chicken served with a sherry cracker stuffing and a rich Boursin cheese sauce. For dessert, take in the Maine sunset over blueberry pie and Shain's ice cream—there's nothing better.

Popular with families and couples alike, the inn's comfortable accommodations are an affordable choice for those wanting to be close to the water. You just have to walk out the front door and across the street to be at the beach. A complimentary continental breakfast with fresh baked muffins, fruit, and juice will send you off right each morning.

The inn's rooms are charmingly varied, but the overall feel is that of a modern motel resort. "That is one of our themes," says Garry. "We have many types of rooms from the small to the very large." (Be sure to specify your sleeping needs—the Hobbit Room is so named for a reason.) The main inn is very much the way it was originally. There really is no changing the structure of a centuries-old building. You may need to wait at the top a staircase for another guest to pass by, and some of the rooms are off narrow and crooked hallways. Some rooms are decorated in a traditional inn style with four-poster beds and quilts, others are larger and more luxuriously appointed and include separate seating areas, spa tubs, or fireplaces. Other historic room options include the inn's Yorkshire and Harbor Crest buildings, which date from 1783 and 1733 respectively and offer pleasantly decorated rooms done in a comfortable, bright cottage style.

As a town first settled in the 1600s, York has a lot of history to explore. The area is often referred to as "the Yorks" and is actually comprised of four communities: York Village, York Harbor, York Beach, and Cape Neddick—home to beloved Nubble Light, which sits on its own island just 100 yards across from Sohier Park and is perhaps Maine's most photographed lighthouse. Meander over to York Village to the Museums of Old York, which manages the town's collection of eight historic properties, some of which date from the early 1700s. Poke around the shops in York Village or follow the Fisherman's Walk along the harbor to admire the show of the ocean. And in the evening retire to the York Harbor Inn and fall asleep to the rhythmic sound of the tide.

480 York Street • York Harbor, ME 03911 • (207) 363-5119 • yorkharborinn.com

NEW HAMPSHIRE

Hancock Inn

ESTABLISHED: 1789

Historic Innkeeping and Late in Life Career Changes

"The Hancock Inn is the oldest inn in New Hampshire. It has been an inn since 1789. The only thing that it knows how to do is be an inn," says Jarvis Coffin of the inn that he and his wife Marcia bought in 2011.

Not only are the Coffins relatively new innkeepers, they are first-time innkeepers after having long careers in media and advertising. And although 24/7 innkeeping can be a challenge for married owners, Jarvis and Marcia are a seasoned entrepreneurial couple. Previous to buying the inn, they worked together for 15 years as owners of an Internet company. Jarvis is the more extroverted half of this innkeeping couple, "We spent 30 to 35 years working hard doing other things. This is another chapter."

Jarvis explains the couple's path to their new profession. "The inn sort of found us. We had been coming back and forth to Hancock for years. My parents live in the area and so do Marcia's. This was the center of gravity for us. My company was in the process of being acquired. And then this property came on the market. We like to cook. We like to entertain. We like historic houses. This is something that we get to do together."

Hancock is as pretty a New England village as you will ever find. It's located in New Hampshire's Monadnock region, in a woodsy valley splashed with lakes and ponds. Hancock itself is tiny with a Main Street that, besides the inn, has only three other full-time businesses: the Hancock General Store, Main Street Cheese, and Fiddleheads Café. With its forests and mountains, the area offers a variety of terrain for the outdoor enthusiast, including skiing Crotched Mountain or paddling Norway Pond. In autumn, there's leaf peeping. As Jarvis says, "There is nothing as spectacular as the foliage in New England. And we are in the heart of it."

The village was incorporated in 1779 and named for John Hancock, owner of the famed large and flowery signature on the Declaration of Independence. At the time John Hancock was one of

The
HANCOCK
INN

CIRCA 1789

the richest men in New England and among his holdings was land in Hillsborough County. Perhaps by honoring Hancock, the new town hoped to attract more citizens and investment. Unfortunately there is no evidence that Hancock ever visited his little New Hampshire namesake town.

But plenty of other people did. And they stayed. As Marcia tells it, "People were looking for a way to start out on their own. And the natural resources of the area beckoned them."

Around this time, Hancock was home to seven taverns, including the Hancock Inn (then Noah Wheeler's inn), built in 1789. By the early 1800s, the inn was known as the Fox Tavern, and Hancock was a stop on the heavily traveled Forest Line Stage between Vermont and Boston. The railroad predominately carried farm produce from northern New England to the city and returned with provisions such as salt, tea, and rum and the latest shop goods. By the mid-1800s, the railroad put an end to the stage business in Hancock, but by then cattle drovers were regularly stopping in town. The herders moved cattle seasonally between Massachusetts and New Hampshire—and the cattle trade is always good business for taverns.

It was in 1915 that the inn was first called the Hancock Hotel. Room renovations at this time led to two important folk art discoveries: a full room landscape mural by itinerant artist Rufus Porter and an original 19th-century wall stencil from famed artist and Hancock resident Moses Eaton.

Today, with its wood floors, fireplaces, and period antiques and reproductions, the inn still radiates the sort of warmth that immediately sets travelers at ease. Jarvis says, "We don't want the spaces to lose anything from its charm and authenticity of being a country inn. The building will take care of some of that for us. It has 200-year-old plumbing. It is drafty. The floors do slope, and the rooms can be small. "

All of the inn's 13 guest rooms are light filled and tastefully decorated in elegant American country-inn style (matelasse coverlets, rustic antiques, and original art), with a wide range of bed sizes from twin to king. Some rooms have gas fireplaces, and others have claw foot tubs or two-person spa tubs.

Modernity is here as well—beds have 600-count sheets and each room has a TV and free Wi-Fi. Man's best friend is welcome here too, as one room is set aside for guests traveling with their dog. In fact, golden retriever host Potter greets every guest with a friendly wag.

Breakfast is included in the room rate and served at individual tables in the sunny back porch. The Hancock Inn kitchen offers freshly squeezed orange juice, seasonal fruit, coffee cake, homemade granola, and a choice of several entrees, including pancakes and local eggs cooked to order, accompanied by a choice of house-made sausage or corned beef hash (or both). They even make their own English muffins.

The Hancock Inn is also a fine dining destination. Dinner is served to both guests and the public seven nights a week from May through October and five nights a week Wednesday through Sunday the rest of the year. Chef Rob Grant has been at the helm for more than a decade, creating menus that feature an array of sustainably-grown food from area farms. Says Jarvis, "We are not trying to reinvent the New England food experience, we just want to be good representatives of it."

Celery root and apple soup with sage oil, autumn squash risotto with dates and goat cheese, and Shaker cranberry pot roast are a few of the items on the ever-changing dining room menu. Rob does simpler fare just as well, including an eight-ounce burger with pork belly, horseradish mayonnaise, and hand-cut fries, or a half of a roasted chicken with potatoes and green beans. Jarvis says that most items on the menu are locally sourced.

Not only is the stewardship of the inn essential to the Coffins' philosophy, but so is the engagement of the Hancock community. Says Marcia, "I think the town was looking for someone to come in, open the doors, and bring in a breath of fresh air. There is also a new owner of the general store. The inn has come back. The town has restored the meetinghouse down the street, and the historic society is newly engaged. Jarvis and I have ambitions of doing a good job and having a nice business, but also to helping to bring energy and excitement to the community. That's been a real driver for us."

On Sunday evenings the innkeeper's supper is a community event. For a very small price, the inn offers a three-course dinner that features a simple main dish such as beef bourguignon or a baked ham along with a salad and dessert. According to Jarvis, "It's been very successful. It's our homage to the community. It's a reminder that this is their clubhouse. That this is their inn. We have never been confused about that. Long after we are gone, we have the expectation that this inn will be here, serving the community, hopefully better than we found it."

33 Main Street • Hancock, New Hampshire • (603) 525-3318 • hancockinn.com

Hanover Inn

ESTABLISHED: 1780

A Once-Colonial-Now-Boutique Inn That Is Ivy League

Located along the Connecticut River in the Upper Valley of New Hampshire and Vermont, the 17th-century town of Hanover was a small farming community inhabited by mostly Connecticut settlers. The town owes its good fortune to the Reverend Eleazar Wheelock, who founded Dartmouth College in 1769. Even today life in this small town revolves around Dartmouth, but with its abundance of cafes, boutiques, and relaxed bars, Hanover also has plenty of off-campus activities to lure travelers and provide for a great weekend getaway.

There is a scholarly dignity to downtown Hanover with its handsome neo-Gothic campus buildings such as the 1928 Baker library and its stately bell tower. Great elms provide dappled shade to the wide expanse of the Green, which is at the geographic and historic heart of Dartmouth life. At the edge of the Green, at the intersection of Wheelock and Main Streets, sits the Hanover Inn, which has long provided accommodation for Dartmouth parents, returning alumni, and those looking to hit the ski slopes of northern New England.

There has been an inn at this corner since 1780, starting with a tavern owned by General Ebenezer Brewster. Originally Brewster's home, the building became an inn when Brewster added the tavern and was charged by the college to provide for "commons board" (room and board) for Dartmouth's students—which numbered around 30 at the time. In 1813, Brewster's Tavern was replaced with a new, larger building by his son Amos and named the Dartmouth Hotel. The Dartmouth Hotel still functioned mostly as boarding for students. With coal- and wood-burning fireplaces and stoves serving as the principal heat source, fire was an ever-present danger in 19th-century New England. The Dartmouth Hotel was no exception, and it burned to the ground in 1887. The site was bought by Dartmouth, and the hotel was quickly rebuilt as a grand five-story, colonial revival brick building with a gabled, dormered roof. It was renamed the Wheelock and opened in 1889.

The hotel has been called the Hanover Inn since the early 1900s, and as Dartmouth grew, so did the inn. The oldest section of the present inn dates from 1924. In 2012 the hotel underwent a $43 million overhaul, transforming it into boutique lodging with 108 luxurious guestrooms and adding Pine, a rustic-meets-modern restaurant and bar.

The inn's current structure mimics the architectural style of the old Wheelock building, blending colonial elements such as a brick exterior and large Palladian windows with a stylistically sophisticated setting. Among the contemporary amenities are alfresco dining on the inn's front patio and an expansive multiuse lobby space that's dominated by a massive granite slab and reclaimed lumber work station, along with a separate lounge area that features a fireplace and several groupings of leather wing chairs.

In the guest rooms, a low-key New England aesthetic prevails with clean-lined, light-colored contemporary furniture and a mix of geometrics and plaid prints in a palette of neutral earth colors of tan, cream, and green. All guest rooms have desk space and excellent task lighting—just in case guests need to crack some books. There is plenty of luxury too, such as marble bathrooms, Gilchrist & Soames products, and large flat-screen televisions.

Pine, the inn's restaurant and bar, is Dartmouth's de facto faculty lounge and the place for dinner on Mom and Dad. On weekends everyone is looking for a scene—and they get one. Boston chef Michael Schlow, named Best Chef in the Northeast by the James Beard Foundation, created the restaurant with Chef Justin Dain. It is designed with lots of windows that offer street-side views of the academic bustle of the Green. The interior combines natural materials: antique barn siding, burnished metal, and granite to lend warmth and familiarity to what is an enormous space. Pine follows a local, seasonal creed with lots of New England–centric dishes. The long bar features a short cocktail list of expertly made, innovative drinks (lots of herb infusions) and a variety of small plates such as spicy kimchi deviled eggs or house-made ricotta crostini with local honey and truffle oil. The simple main courses are the best. Choose from a satisfying roast chicken with roasted vegetables or prime rib with potato puree and corn. And as befitting a restaurant that caters to a college crowd, they offer a fine, flavorful burger that comes with a pile of french fries and sriracha aioli.

Today's Hanover Inn is as pedigreed as the school it serves, and it attracts an impressive clientele of academics, dignitaries, celebrities, and politicians—especially in presidential primary years. New Hampshire holds the first primary in the nation, and nearly every candidate visits Dartmouth during that time.

The inn's location is also ideal for the culturally minded traveler. The inn is adjacent to Dartmouth's Hood Museum of Art—its Assyrian ninth-century BCE stone reliefs are among its most treasured holdings. The Hopkins Center for the Arts, or "the Hop," is connected to the inn as well and serves as the cultural hub not just of Dartmouth but also all of Hanover. Performances span dance, music, stage, and cinema, and many are open to the public.

Hanover is essentially a border town. Norwich, Vermont, with its Montshire Science Museum and the nation's oldest flour company, King Arthur, and its flagship baker's store (founded in 1790), is a two-minute drive across the Connecticut River. Recreation in Hanover tends to be of the outdoors variety. There is paddling the Connecticut River, cross-country and downhill skiing minutes away, and the area is laced with hiking trails—a part of the Appalachian trail cuts right through town.

Two East Wheelock • Hanover, NH 03755 • (603) 643-4300 • hanoverinn.com

Three Chimney's Inn and ffrost Sawyer Tavern

CIRCA: 1649

A Historic Lodging and Dining Destination In Its Own Right

In the quiet of the 18th century, the rumble of mighty mill wheels turning along the river could be heard throughout what is today the seacoast town of Durham, New Hampshire. Today you hear the noise of a college town bustling with academic life—an excess of inexpensive eateries, coffee shops, and, as you would expect, a rather lively nightlife scene.

Located in southeastern New Hampshire, just 30 miles from the Massachusetts border, Durham is home to the University of New Hampshire (UNH). Just a mile from campus and Main Street sits the Three Chimney's Inn. Known for generations of Durham residents as the Frost Homestead, the original building dates from 1649 and is one of the oldest residential structures in the state.

The sprawling yellow clapboard, two-and-a-half-story house itself is wonderfully sited with expansive formal gardens and a reflecting pond on a promontory that overlooks the Oyster River and Mill Falls. It was likely the building's advantageous location that saved it from destruction by Native Americans in 1694 during what has become known as the Raid on Oyster River. A dozen other dwellings of the frontier village were not so lucky and were burned to the ground. Nearly 100 residents were killed or captured.

This territory along the banks of the Oyster River was once home to ancient native settlements and, in the 1630s, to a small number of English settlers. In early colonial times there was a lot of economic opportunity in this region. Pioneers made their livings through farming, fishing, and the lumber trade. It is here that the mouth of the Oyster River meets Great Bay, an estuary that connects with the Piscataqua River and eventually the Atlantic Ocean. It was a river system ideal for trade and transportation.

Valentine Hill, a pioneer originally from Boston, saw an opportunity. In 1649 he obtained a grant for the land near the falls of the Oyster River and broke ground. He built the original

homestead for what is now the Three Chimney's Inn. By 1651 he had constructed both a sawmill and a gristmill and owned 500 acres of surrounding land. Valentine Hill became a wealthy man, and his descendents lived in the home for many years.

The original house was a simple, one-story, one-room structure with a center chimney and a summer kitchen in the basement. By 1700, a substantial expansion by Valentine's son Nathaniel included a two-story kitchen wing, which reconfigured the first floor to have two flanking parlors, and added upstairs bedrooms. Today, guests enter the inn through this addition into the Coppers Dining Room, the homestead's original room, with its massive brick fireplace and wide-plank floors.

As the Hill family's fortune grew, so too did the house, acquiring several additions, most notably a barn in 1795. In the early 1800s the house was purchased and substantially enlarged by George Frost, a merchant and shipbuilder. The grounds and gardens were greatly expanded by James and Margaret Frost Pepperall Sawyer (descendants of Frost) in the early 1900s, when the house was converted into a summer home for their large family.

In 1996, the property was acquired by Sagamore Hill, a company that is owned by Marcy Carsey, the Emmy Award–winning producer of *The Cosby Show*, *Roseanne*, and *Third Rock from the Sun*. Marcy graduated from the University of New Hampshire in 1966 with a degree in English and is one of the university's best-known and active benefactors. Says Karen Meyer, the Three Chimney's innkeeper, "Marcy has a real love for Durham."

After a total restoration, the inn opened to guests in 1998. Says Karen, "Before, the inn was in ruins. And for a time, the building was a frat house. To this day, we still get guests who tell us that they used to live here or came to a party here. They are always very vivid remembrances!"

The inn's 23 rooms are exactly what one would expect, and want, from a historic New England inn. One of the coziest rooms to book is the Theodore Roosevelt room in the carriage house. It has a hunter's theme and Edwardian charm in a color scheme of sage and burnished red, a four-post queen bed draped in a leopard print, antique Oriental rug, a gas fireplace, and an oversized soaking tub.

Whatever room you book, be sure to leave time to wander the inn's gardens and downtown Durham. Or head over to Portsmouth, just 15 miles away, for a wonderful mix of funk and charm, thanks to its boutiques and cafes.

Or, if you prefer to stick closer to home, check out the inn's ffrost Sawyer Tavern, a handsome wood-worn spot in which UNH students pack nightly for craft beers and appetizers prepared with

flair, such as pork belly BLT bites and grilled oysters with horseradish butter. If you're not feeling adventurous, order the potato-crusted haddock—it's been on the menu for more than 20 years for good reason. Oh, and if you've had too much to drink, don't think you're seeing double. The tavern's quirky spelling of ffrost? In earlier times, printers used double lower-case "fs" to denote a capital "F."

That's not the only piece of the past the inn can claim. Even though the Hill family is long gone from the house, one member is said to remain. "I've felt someone put their hand on my shoulder, but no one was around," says Karen. "Doors lock by themselves, there are noises in rooms that don't have guests. There are some things that happen here that you really can't

explain." It is suspected that the spirit of Hannah Hill, one of Valentine Hill's daughters, is the culprit. She is said to have died an early death by drowning in the Oyster River. But don't worry, Karen says Hannah is a friendly ghost.

Ghost or no ghost, be aware that the inn is always sold out (and with a waitlist) well in advance for UNH events, especially move-in, family, and commencement weekends. Be sure to make plans accordingly.

17 Newmarket Road • Durham, New Hampshire 03824 • (603) 868-7800 • threechimneysinn.com

VERMONT

The Dorset Inn

ESTABLISHED 1796

Sleepy Vermont Town, Wonderfully Comfortable Rooms, and Stellar Dining

More than two centuries have passed since folks first hitched horses off the white columned porch and crossed the threshold of the Dorset Inn. Built in 1796, the inn has always served as the cornerstone of Dorset civic life. In the evening, travelers would dine together at the inn's public table and then spend time in front of a fire, generously passing drinks and news from around New England before retiring to their rooms. All manner of subjects were discussed, especially politics. In colonial times the territory that would eventually be Vermont was constantly in dispute—claimed by both the Province of New York and the Province of New Hampshire.

Dorset, a quiet hamlet founded in 1761, is tucked within a high valley of south-central Vermont. To the east are the distant hills of the Green Mountains. To the west are New York's Taconic Mountains. And off to the north looms Dorset Mountain, recalling bygone days when marble quarrying was the area's principal industry. The town's marble sidewalks were first laid in the 1870s and are still a treasured feature. Dorset marble was used in building both the New York Public Library and Harvard Medical School.

Today a thriving arts scene and tourism are the pillars of the town's economy. The Dorset Playhouse brings in thousands of people each year for its professional productions by its resident stock company. Tourists come for Dorset's quaint tranquility and enjoy the outdoors by hiking the Appalachian Trail or fishing, canoeing, and kayaking the Battenkill. There are also several golf courses and two ski areas, Bromley and Stratton, nearby.

The Dorset Inn, situated on the town's green, proudly claims that it is the oldest continuously operated inn in Vermont. Through the centuries, the Dorset Inn has seen countless owners. Interestingly, among the inn's more noteworthy proprietors are two women entrepreneurs. Amy Ann Lapham owned the inn from 1917 through 1938, and was responsible for the inn's first major expansion, raising the roof over the ballroom to add more guest rooms. From 1985 through 2008, Chef Sissy Hicks

owned the inn. She is still considered by many to be a leader of the Vermont-grown, organic dining movement. Since 2008, the Dorset Inn has been owned by husband and wife hoteliers, Steve and Lauren Bryant. The Bryants are responsible for the inn's most recent refurbishment, including a refresh of the inn's common areas and guestrooms.

The Dorset Inn's dining room and tavern have loyal fans who have been coming back for decades along with a new generation of customers drawn by a fresh and local food philosophy that creates flavors that are crisp and clean.

Many Dorset Inn regulars book their vacations here because of the phenomenal staff. Cindy Bebee has been a waitress at the Dorset Inn since 1972. Soft spoken, Cindy quietly rules the inn's breakfast room, taking orders, serving food, and tidying up. "I'm from Rupert, right over the hill," she says. "I started right after high school. I really like working here."

According to Cindy, the inn has a resident spirit named The General. "He's in a Civil War uniform," she says. "I've seen him a couple of times, once at the bar, another time in the dining room with a woman and child. He's a friendly ghost." The uniform makes sense, as the inn is believed to have been a stop on the Underground Railroad, helping slaves escape to Canada.

Cindy's colleague Nuni Ragonese has been at the Dorset Inn since 1986. Brash and blousy Nuni holds forth in the tavern chatting up the regulars. "I came here from Connecticut in 1969 to learn to ski, and stayed. Every day is fun. I still entertain people. I want to make the Dorset Inn a place that people come back to. Now I get fourth generation guests." Together, Cindy and Nuni connect with their customers and with each other. The Dorset Inn is lucky to have them both.

As tastes, appetites, and expectations have changed, so too have the inn's dining options. Today, the wood-paneled, clubby tavern is more popular than the dining room, especially for locals. The menus are determined largely around what is available from local farmers, foragers, and fishermen. In the spring that means rhubarb, watercress, and bass. In the winter you'll find split pea and ham soup and roasted duck with currant compote. But some things, Nuni says, will never change. "People are still ordering calves liver with onions and the turkey croquettes."

Each of the inn's 25 charming, antique-filled rooms is unique; some have fireplaces, others separate living rooms. The best rooms overlook the green. All of the inn's bathrooms have recently been renovated and upgraded in a classic, traditional style. In a nod to the area's marble tradition, the bathrooms feature white marble mosaic floors, subway tile walls, and polished chrome hardware. Some of the larger baths feature whirlpools.

In any case, as an overnight guest you'll wake up to a dreamy Vermont breakfast. Among the choices on the menu—ultra-fluffy buttermilk pancakes with warm local maple syrup and thick-cut bacon; house-cured corned beef with perfectly poached eggs and hollandaise sauce; or a delicate goat cheese and herb omelet with toast.

Breakfast here is warm, simple, and cozy—like the inn itself. In search of the perfect New England inn? The Dorset Inn may just be it.

8 Church Street • Dorset, VT 05251 • (802) 867-5500 • dorsetinn.com

The Equinox

ESTABLISHED: 1769

Vintage Vermont Luxe

The jaw-dropping scenery of Southern Vermont's unspoiled Battenkill River Valley has helped to make bucolic Manchester an outdoorsman's playground and travel destination since the mid-1800s. Mount Equinox is also a major draw, being one of the highest mountains in Vermont. It was named by Captain William Partridge, Vermont's surveyor general, who climbed to the top of the peak around the time of the autumnal equinox (when day and night are nearly equal) on September 19, 1823. The five-mile Skyline Drive toll road is still one of the best summit drives in New England—with a commanding mountain view of Massachusetts, New York, and New Hampshire, and, on a very clear day, Canada.

Named for the mountain, The Equinox Inn, made famous by its association with the Orvis family (of fly fishing business fame), is Manchester's most well known property. With its fluted columned façade facing Manchester Village Square, it makes a stunning impression.

And while the spirit of this mountain retreat harkens back to a modest Revolutionary-era tavern, this is a modern, contemporary resort. You really don't ever have to leave: there's a spa with indoor pool, tennis, and golf, not to mention several casual and fine dining options on the property. For most, Vermont's rustic scenery is the draw: there's the silhouette of Mount Equinox right out the hotel's back door along with sparkling ponds and acres of farmland just minutes away.

Chances are, you could probably describe the very same scene at the Equinox fifty years or even a century ago. Richard Hom is the resort's chief concierge. He presides over all from his desk in the front window alcove—really the nerve center of guest operations at the hotel. "Most of our guests, in my mind, want calm, serenity, and to get back to nature," he says. "They are coming to the Equinox for a respite."

Richard reveals that many guests ask about "the Equinox story." The hotel's history is on display everywhere, from the enlarged archival photos that line the hallways to the inn's carefully preserved architecture, such as the Chop House dining room's polished wide plank floors and its great marble fireplace chiseled with "L.C. Orvis 1832."

Equinox history runs deep, back to 1769 when the Marsh Tavern occupied roughly the spot of the hotel's Chop House restaurant. Established by William Marsh, a prosperous Vermont landowner and Torie sympathizer, the original tavern and inn welcomed thirsty out-of-town travelers on cart or horse.

The inn, some claim, played a crucial part in the laying of the groundwork for the state of Vermont. Ethan Allen—and his image of rugged individualism—is dear to Vermonters. The Revolutionary War hero, who led the fight at the Battle of Ticonderoga, also created the local militia force known as the "Green Mountain Boys." The "Boys," headed by Ethan Allen's younger brother Ira, established a "Council of Safety" to raise money for the fledgling republic. The council gathered at Marsh Tavern to discuss the idea of confiscating and selling property owned by British Loyalists. It's not entirely clear whether Marsh Tavern was one of those expropriations, but what is known is that William Marsh fled north to Canada, and by 1780, Thaddeus Munson purchased the property, eventually expanding it and renaming it Munson's Inn.

The inn passed through several owners until the early 1800s when it was bought by Franklin Orvis, son of Levi Church Orvis, a local merchant and member of Manchester's most prominent family. In 1853 his son Franklin Orvis consolidated the family's homestead with the family store to create the 65-room Equinox House. Franklin's brother Charles would later establish the Orvis fly fishing company, forever linking the family name with the town of Manchester.

With the advent of the railroad, Equinox House evolved into a summer retreat for the well-heeled, gentrified crowd, who came for weeks at a time to escape the heat of the cities and to enjoy rest and recreation in the cool Green Mountain air. Favorite pastimes included hiking, fishing, and golfing. They would have their meals—and they were huge meals—in the Equinox dining rooms. Among the interesting selections on the menu in the early 1900s were mutton chops, codfish balls, and honeycomb tripe.

A relic of those halcyon days, the hotel's lobby scale is on exhibit in the Equinox spa. Richard says "A hundred and fifty years ago, guests would weigh themselves when they checked in and when they checked out. If guests relaxed and ate well, they gained weight and the hotel was doing a good job." At this time, too, the healing properties of mineral spring water was all the rage. The hotel opened the Equinox Spring Bottling Company to meet the needs of guests who wanted to take cases home as a souvenir.

Franklin Orvis's hotel became one of the most popular New England summer mountain resorts. The hotel became especially famous after a visit from President Lincoln's wife, Mary Todd Lincoln, who stayed at the hotel with their sons Robert and Tad during the summer of 1864. The

Civil War was still raging, so the President didn't join them. But Robert, Lincoln's only son to survive to adulthood, eventually settled in Vermont, building his summer home, Hildene, just down the road from the Equinox. Presidents Ulysses Grant, Benjamin Harrison, Theodore Roosevelt, and William Howard Taft are also all said to have stayed here.

The hotel's fall from grace was gradual: the advent of the automobile, two World Wars, and the Depression all took their toll. By the 1970s the hotel fell into bankruptcy, needing lots of cash and renovations to make a comeback. Eventually the hotel reopened in 1985 after millions of dollars in structural overhauls, including the addition of an expansive 13,000-square-foot-spa complex that features endless views of Mount Equinox.

Today the Equinox is a true four-season resort with an award-winning eighteen-hole golf course and Bromley ski mountain just down the road. Looking for adventure? How about taking a test drive at the Land Rover Driving School? Maybe try fly-fishing or shooting lessons with Orvis instructors? Or experience the thrill of falconry? The list of activities at the Equinox is impressive to say the least.

Food is also a big part of the Equinox experience. The resort has five restaurants and bars, including farm-to-table dining at Marsh Tavern and the Chop House, a bustling dining room that features expertly cooked beef and top-notch sides. The hotel's Falcon bar maintains a hide-away ambiance with a dark, distressed wood interior and an impressive selection of whiskeys.

According to Richard, "What makes the Equinox so enticing is that it is a destination rich with history. There are things to do here that are not really offered anywhere else. Besides, it's just really pretty here too."

3567 Main Street • Manchester Village, VT 05254 • (877) 854-7625 • equinoxresort.com

Grafton Inn

ESTABLISHED: 1801

A Quaint Vermont Village Where No One Locks the Door

In this corner of New England, the dirt road still reigns. In the foothills of the Green Mountains, it's a longer than expected drive off the interstate along Route 121. And then the pavement ends. You will meander slowly along an eight-mile, unpaved stretch of road through dense old-growth forest to reach Grafton, a picture-perfect village of just 600 residents in central southern Vermont.

The Grafton Inn is the heart of the village, its wide-columned, rocking-chair-strewn front porch calling you to sit and enjoy a view of the stream-fed swimming pond across the road.

Everywhere in Grafton there are rural vistas to please the eye. Its earliest pioneers (mostly from Massachusetts and Connecticut) were farmers attracted to the availability of inexpensive, hilly farmland. That same rolling green countryside is said to have inspired the writing of Rudyard Kipling, who lived in the area from 1892 to 1896.

You can still sense the serenity of the village from its early days by strolling down folksy Main Street, past the small shops and the clutch of 18th- and 19th-century houses grouped around the white, steepled church.

Located along the Saxtons River and founded in 1754 as part of the territory of New Hampshire, the town was originally named Thomlinson. According to local lore, the naming rights for the town were sold in 1791 to Joseph Axtell, who renamed it after his hometown of Grafton, Massachusetts, for the high bid of $5 and a jug of rum.

The Grafton Inn began life in the years after the Revolutionary War. As early as 1788, Samuel Spring had a tavern license for the house on this property. The original two-story brick structure on this site dates from 1795 and belonged to Enos Lovell, who chose to convert his home to a stagecoach stop in 1801. The inn is ideally located at the junction of two stage coach routes: the north-south route from Montreal to Boston and the east-west route from the Maine and New Hampshire coasts to Albany.

The property changed hands many times over the years and was substantially enlarged. In 1865 the Phelps brothers bought the inn and ran it for nearly 50 years. The inn's fortune's mirrored the town's. By the 19th century, Grafton was a prosperous community; sheep farming, logging, and soapstone quarrying were the town's principal early enterprises. By the 1900s however, the town—and the inn—were struggling.

Fast-forward to 1963 and the inn, then known as the Old Tavern, was desperately in need of attention. Thanks largely to the non-profit Windham Foundation, the village of Grafton is a historic preservation success story. Created in 1963 by New York investment banker and Princeton resident Dean Mathey, the Windham Foundation strives to "promote the vitality of Grafton and Vermont's rural communities." Mathey had summered in Grafton as a boy, and the foundation was his attempt to save the town and preserve the Vermont way of life. According to Bob Allen, the CEO and President of the Windham Foundation, "Mathey, along with his cousin Mat Hall, decided that they wanted to invest a substantial amount of money in Grafton. The Windham Foundation was initially funded with $24 million. That was a lot of money back then."

The first project of the Windham Foundation was to renovate the inn. In the early 1960s the Grafton Inn was an eleven-room hotel with only two bathrooms and chamber pots in all the rooms. "I like to remind people that this was in 1963, not 1863," says Bob.

The inn became a much larger property with the addition of several village properties. Today, the Grafton Inn has a total of 44 rooms, including several stand-alone guest homes ideal for families or groups. The guest rooms are historic and romantic in equal measure and feature period wallpapers, four-poster beds, and a mix of folk and fine American antiques. "No two rooms are close to being alike," says Bob. Rooms don't have televisions and there is spotty Wi-Fi, encouraging guests to slow down, but at least every guest room has a private bathroom today.

The inn is acclaimed for its country breakfast. Each morning begins with offerings such as challah bread french toast with maple syrup and eggs scrambled with roasted seasonal vegetables and goat cheese, served with home fries and toast.

After your hearty breakfast and a day of exploring, return to the inn for a late lunch or dinner at Phelps Barn Pub. Attached to the main inn, Phelps Barn is a beauty. The soaring two-story space is actually three different barns that have been cobbled together. It serves as the inn's principal casual dining space and features a down-home menu of comfort foods that includes a chicken ciabatta with applewood bacon, baked macaroni with a two-year aged cheddar cheese sauce, and steak frites.

Full-scale fine dining is available at the inn's Old Tavern restaurant, where you'll find a resolutely farm-to-table menu featuring Vermont farmers and food artisans. The charcuterie board includes assorted local cheeses, apricot chutney, and dried figs. For the main dish choose from such creations as pistachio trout with calico rice and buttered turnips, or filet mignon served with rosemary merlot butter, mashed potatoes, and roasted garlic creamed spinach. Sweets (also served at Phelps Barn) include a flourless chocolate torte and a caramel pumpkin bread pudding with toasted pecans, but the cast-iron baked chocolate chip cookie with homemade ice cream is the must.

When guests arrive at the Grafton Inn, they receive a welcome gift of Grafton cheese with crackers, and you will notice that Grafton cheese is a prominent ingredient in many dishes in the inn's two restaurants. This is thanks to another successful project by the Windham Foundation. They stepped forward to restart the Grafton Cheese Company, which had existed in the village from 1892 until it burned in a 1912 fire. Grafton Cheese is still made at the production facility right up the street from the inn. Visitors are invited to watch the cheese-making process through the large viewing windows.

The Grafton Pond Recreation Center is another Windham Foundation project. The 2,000-acre property represents Vermont at its outdoorsy best, with cross-country skiing, ice-skating, and dog sledding in the winter, and hiking, mountain biking, canoeing, and fly-fishing the rest of the year. Inn guests have full access and free rentals of bikes and ski equipment.

Grafton is certainly a one-company town. In addition to the houses that are part of the inn, the Windham Foundation owns a lot of residential and commercial properties in town. Every time a house in need of repair became available, the foundation bought it, fixed it up, and leased it (often for below-market rates) to someone in the community.

According to Bob, "There is a misconception about the foundation; a lot of people believe that the foundation has been established just to serve the village of Grafton. Annually we give out grants to rural communities throughout Vermont for historic preservation, youth services, and agriculture. All to help keep Vermont's small communities running."

The foundation's hard work has certainly paid off. Perhaps a thought of thanks would be appropriate as you curl up in a wing chair in front of the fireplace in Grafton Inn's charming parlor with a book and a glass of wine.

---

92 Main Street • Grafton, Vermont 05146 • (802) 234-8702 • graftoninnvermont.com

Ye Olde Tavern

ESTABLISHED: 1790

Sometimes Flavor Is More Than Just What Is on the Plate

Dating from 1790, Ye Olde Tavern is actually Vermont's oldest inn. With its stately pillared entrance and large barn—18th century inns needed substantial stabling for horses and wagons—Ye Olde Tavern certainly looks the part.

The distinctive three-story ochre clapboard building was constructed by well-known Dorset builder Aaron Sheldon and was originally named the Stagecoach Inn. Standing as it does on Main Street in Manchester, it was a popular stop on the busy Boston to Albany route during the 19th century.

"This marble was quarried from Danby, two mountain ranges over," owner Michael Brandt proudly says, pointing to the large hearth in what was the property's original tavern.

A native of New York, Michael has lived in Vermont since 1995. He knows quite a bit about his building's history and describes how in the early years of the tavern there was boarding for travelers on the second floor while travelers danced the night away on the third floor, where the tavern has a rare-for-its-time "spring floor" ballroom.

In the mid-1800s, as the Green Mountains became a popular summer destination, the tavern expanded to have as many as 20 bedrooms. It was at this time that the full-width marble porch was added, giving a touch of class to what was then known as Lockwood's Hotel. Later, the property was known as Thayer's Hotel. By the early 1900s it was called the Fairview Hotel, but it had seen better days, and was eventually closed.

The tavern stood vacant for many years. It still lacked electricity when it was bought and renovated by Walter Clemons McGuire, who operated the building as both a boarding house and antiques store from the early 1940s through the 1970s.

Today, the tavern's pleasingly decorated dining rooms feature many antiques and curios from Walter's collection, including Harvard pennants (Walter was a Harvard man), blue and white

transfer ware, and antique wall clocks. The low-ceilinged rooms wander off in several directions and have slightly slanted wide-planked floors.

Of course, no old New England tavern would be complete without a ghost in residence. Some diners have reported the presence of a pipe-smoking spirit said to possibly be Walter. Michael, however, is not so sure. "I personally think there is an explanation for every sound and sighting."

The name "Olde Tavern" has been on the building since Walter's time. The "Ye" is a legacy of the 1976 bicentennial, added when the property was bought and renovated by Peter Palmer and became a full-time restaurant.

Michael and his wife Minna were proprietors of a well-known Manchester breakfast restaurant when they bought the tavern in 2001. They soon sold the breakfast spot to focus on the tavern. Over the years, the Brandts have succeeded in marrying favorite New England fare with a contemporary twist. Together they have created one of the most atmospheric dining rooms in all of New England with its flickering candlelight, Moses Eaton–style-stencil-trimmed walls, and nicely spaced linen-draped tables.

Chef Clifton Cooper has been with the Brandts from the beginning, overseeing the preparation of standbys such as prime rib and chicken pot pie while bringing new fans to dishes like crispy duck with a blackberry demi-glace. Friday night venison nights and mid-week lobster "palooza" nights are hugely popular local weekly dining events. Cranberry fritters with maple butter arrive at the table before every meal, and many diners purchase a mason jar of maple butter to take home.

Care for a drink? In keeping with colonial tavern tradition, there's a fine selection of cider and mead along with several vintage brandy- or rum-focused cocktails. Michael is extremely proud that the tavern has received the Wine Spectator award of excellence every year since 2003. The tavern's wine and beer list includes bottles from Vermont's Charlotte Village Winery and a tasty 1790 Ale made especially for the restaurant by Vermont favorite Long Trail Brewery.

There's always a good turnout of locals and visitors taking advantage of the tavern's early-bird special from 5:00 to 6:00 p.m., Sunday through Friday. Diners can choose from several of the tavern's classics, including the Yankee pot roast with mashed potatoes or the shrimp scampi served with rice pilaf along with a salad, dessert, and coffee for a very modest sum.

Foliage season is the busiest at the tavern. "We open the second floor to accommodate the overflow. Most of our customers are from Boston or Manhattan, but in the fall we also get a lot of international visitors from Canada, Europe, and Asia," explains Michael.

When asked about the tavern's role in Manchester history Michael doesn't hesitate. "It's a neat old building, and it's a little rough around the edges, but it's a landmark in Manchester. Although we can't say that George Washington was here. And neither, unfortunately, was Ethan Allen, we are glad to be maintaining the traditions here."

5183 Main Street • Manchester, VT 05255 • (802) 362-0611 • yeoldetavern.net

CONNECTICUT

Captain Daniel Packer Inne

ESTABLISHED: 1756

Waterfront Colonial Watering Hole

"Sometimes I think I am living in a postcard. You have the drawbridge over the river, the church on the hill, and the sailboats in the sound," says Allie Kiley Nasin, owner of the Captain Daniel Packer Inne, a restaurant and tavern located in Mystic, Connecticut. This sprawling gambrel-roof Dutch Colonial was built by its namesake, Captain Daniel Packer, a sea captain and Patriot during the Revolutionary War. While the building is certainly antique, the food and drinks are totally current.

Located along Connecticut's "Gold Coast," just south of Rhode Island, Mystic is the quintessential small New England coastal town. Boutiques and restaurants, along with gracious Colonial and Federal Homes (many with water views), line the sidewalk of the main street. An 85-foot span of the Mystic River Bascule Bridge swings skyward hourly, stopping traffic to allow for the passing of recreational boats. It's an everyday reminder that the rhythm of life here is still tied to the sea.

Perched at the mouth of the Mystic River just before it flows into Long Island Sound, the area is prime for inhabitants to make their livings from the water. Both the river and the town take their name from the native Pequot word mis-si-tuk, meaning "little river running to the sea." The Dutch and English settlers built the first commercial wharves for fishermen and boat makers here as early as the 1650s.

In 1754 Captain Daniel Packer had acquired a large land grant along the banks of the Mystic River and established his family farm. He also built a rudimentary rope ferry to serve stagecoach travelers along the Boston Post Road as well as to transport goods and livestock across the Mystic River between the village and the farms to the east. By 1756 Packer's business ventures included an inn and tavern, where he held forth nightly, recounting his exploits on the high seas to a captive audience.

By the War of 1812, Daniel Packer's descendants' entrepreneurial endeavors would not only include farming and innkeeping, but shipbuilding too. However, by the 1820s the invention of the

steamboat, and later, the advent of the railroad, sent Mystic's fortunes into a long, slow decline. The Packer family adjusted yet again. Packer's Pine Tar Soap was invented in 1867 and was manufactured in Mystic until 1967. Today Packer's Pine Tar Soap is considered an American heritage brand. It's still manufactured—although now from a factory in New Jersey. Its distinctive manly outdoorsy scent still has legions of loyal users.

The Packer homestead stayed in the family for several generations. However, according to Allie, as the Packer children grew up and moved away, smaller sections of the house were occupied while the rest of the building was falling apart. By the 1970s the house was deserted; the building was dilapidated, and there were trees growing through the windows.

There were "No Trespassing" signs out front when Allie's parents, Richard and Lulu Kiley, rescued the property in 1979 with the intention of restoring the building and converting the site to a restaurant. An extensive remodel was carried out with an emphasis on historic preservation. It turned out to be an informed renovation. Much of the inn's interior woodwork is original, including the beams, fireplace mantles, and sloping wood floors. As Allie explains, "My father was a visionary. He had a unique combination of business sense and creativity. He wanted to keep the integrity of the building. Anything that he could keep, he did."

In fact, he may have kept more than he bargained for. A Packer niece named Ada passed away in the house of scarlet fever in 1873 at the age of seven. It is said that she still likes to play in the stairwell and is best described as mischievous. Allie says Ada's presence is most often felt when there are other children dining at the inn.

Allie takes it all in stride, having been the manager of the Daniel Parker Inn since her father's passing in 2001. Over the years, she has been at the forefront of promoting the Connecticut wine and beer industry. During the recession in 2007 she started a weekly Sunday event offering half-off bottles of wine made by local growers such as Jonathan Edwards Winery and Stonington Vineyards, and half-off local draft beers from places such as Cottrell Brewing and Outer Light. "I have never stopped the promotion. It's my way of supporting Connecticut wineries and breweries. I want these places to stay around; I think they are a great attraction to the area."

Upstairs, the inn offers a fine dining experience with gracious service and a menu of regional dishes that strongly emphasizes local seafood. You can't go wrong with dishes such as baked Stonington Bomster scallops with white wine or lobster ravioli in a tarragon cream sauce.

Dark and delightful, the downstairs pub has been part of Mystic life and commerce for more than two centuries. Here you'll find hearty dishes such as wild boar sausage chili and fish and chips

as well as nightly live music for the regular late-night drinking crowd. In both the pub and dining room you can order lemon pepper chicken finished in a beurre blanc sauce. "It's a staple," says Allie. "At one point it came off the menu, but people like it so much, it had to go back on."

Everyone who comes to Mystic seems to eventually end up at the inn, or DPI, as the locals affectionately call it. It's the place to be in Mystic after a Connecticut College football game or a day of sailing or touring. DPI is a legacy that Allie continues to carry on for her family. She is her father's daughter. "This used to be Mystic's bad side of the tracks. Thirty years ago, these buildings were falling down. My dad came here and other people started to invest in the area. Now all of Water Street is much more business friendly and vibrant because of him."

32 Water Street • Mystic, CT 06355 • (860) 536-3555 • danielpacker.com

Griswold Inn

ESTABLISHED: 1776

Throwing it Back to 1776

Of all the colonial-era watering holes in New England, few approach the legendary status of the Griswold Inn. For a beautiful coastal New England setting, Essex, Connecticut is hard to beat. Originally called Potapoug and settled in 1648, Essex was, until the 1850s, part of the nearby town of Saybrook.

Halfway between Boston and New York, Essex is located on the banks of the Connecticut River, five miles inland from Long Island Sound. Its Main Street is lined with Federal homes. Antiques stores and art galleries seem to tumble down to the town marina, which is filled with sailboats and yachts. In the summer, the town's scenic waterfront park hosts outdoor concerts and a farmer's market.

Originally a farming community, the town shifted its economic focus by the 18th century to shipbuilding. In its heyday, between the Revolutionary and Civil Wars, Essex shipyards built as many as 600 ships of all types, including fishing, trade, and war.

The impetus for the establishment of the Griswold Inn was the building of the Revolutionary warship the *Oliver Cromwell*. In January of 1776, Essex shipbuilder Uriah Hayden received a contract from the colony of Connecticut to build the full-rigged schooner. Uriah's shipyard was at the foot of Main Street, and he built a tavern/inn close by to accommodate shipbuilders and sailors. As owner Joan Paul explains, "The Gris opened in June of 1776 as exactly what we do today."

The Griswold Inn, or "the Gris" (pronounced Griz) as it is lovingly known by locals, is owned and operated by the Paul family of Essex. In 1993 Geoff Paul, an amateur art historian, was discussing with then owner, Bill Winterer, the possibility of purchasing a Guy Wiggins painting of the inn. Bill reportedly said, "Why buy the painting, when you can buy the real thing?" And so, the Paul family bought the Griswold Inn. Geoff, along with brothers Greg and Doug are investment partners in the business; Doug and his wife Joan are involved in the inn's day-to-day operation.

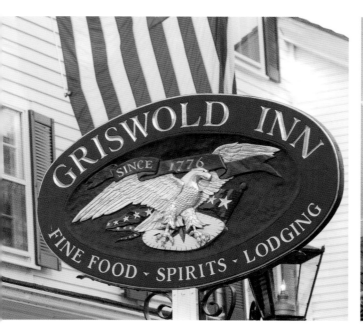

Says Joan, "The Connecticut River is one of the only rivers on the East Coast that is not industrialized. There is a sandbar at its mouth, so you can't have big cargo ships here. That's why [Essex] still looks like an 18th-century town."

A big part of the small town's charm is its many annual parades. For every season there is a celebration in Essex. The summer kicks off with a Memorial Day parade of marching veterans and flag-festooned antique cars. The very popular Dogs on the Dock parade takes place in the fall. In the winter there is the Essex Holiday Stroll when the whole town is set aglow with lights and lanterns. In the spring, Essex patriotism is on full display for the Burning of the Ships Day/Loser Day celebration, which commemorates the British Raid of Essex on April 8, 1814, when the British torched 27 newly built American ships in the harbor.

Essex is one of the few American towns to have been attacked by a foreign power. Soon after, the British commandeered the Griswold Inn as a base of operations. As a nod to the inn's connection to the raid, it serves a traditional English Hunt Breakfast every Sunday from 11 a.m. to 1 p.m. in its historic dining rooms. And unlike some New England inns geared toward creating a historic atmosphere, the food is not an afterthought. The dinner menu features Yankee fare such as roasted cod with a butter crumb crust and braised short ribs with whipped potatoes, but also modern New England cuisine that is smart and seasonal, such as maple-glazed scallops and a skillet-seared pork chop with cider jus and roasted fingerlings.

If fine dining is not what you are in the mood for, the inn offers pub fare in the Tap Room, which really is the soul of the Griswold Inn. Originally built in 1738 as an Essex schoolhouse, it was moved here and added to the inn in 1801. An indefinable ambiance makes the Tap Room a comfortable homeport for everyone, especially for anyone bewitched by the song of the sea.

The Tap Room's domed ceiling of crushed oyster shells mixed with horsehair is darkened with the rich patina of years of tobacco and firewood smoke. Old ship's lanterns light the space, which is dominated by a large mahogany carved bar and a charmingly ramshackle interior that features a pot-bellied stove topped with a year-round Christmas tree and wood-paneled walls.

And for those who enjoy sailing songs or drinking songs (really one and the same), Monday Sea Chantey Night in the Tap Room is a must. Chanteys were work songs of the sea during the age of sail—rousing tales of maidens, ale, and days plundering and pillaging. Sea Chantey Night has been a Gris tradition since the 1970s. This is an all-in sing-along, but no experience is necessary to join in the chorus. "You would think it is old people, but it is not," says Joan. "It's mostly twenty-somethings. Everybody knows the words to the songs. It's almost a cult following."

If neither of these experiences appeals to you, there's yet another option of contemporary dining that attracts a younger, more urban crowd in the inn's Wine Bar, a more sophisticated space where the knowledgeable staff will guide you through the ordering process of the by-the-glass wines and a menu designed for sharing. Of course, that glass of Chateauneuf de Pape is only as good as the polenta pizza and the confit duck breast with which it is paired, which, thanks to Chef David Mitchel, are superb.

Throughout the inn, the history of Essex is crammed into every nook and cranny with gold-framed paintings of boats and the sea, half-hull boat models, nautical maps, and other artifacts. There are works by household names such as Norman Rockwell and Currier & Ives as well as noted American ship portrait painters John Bard and Antonio Jacobsen. "We have the largest private collection of maritime art in the country. A lot of these pieces should be in a museum behind velvet ropes, but here they are accessible," says Joan.

Aside from great food and fantastic history, the inn also offers accommodations that include 33 rooms spread throughout several buildings on both sides of Main Street. The rooms have a homey, hideaway quality and are decorated with antiques and fine reproductions. Some have fireplaces and/or water views. There is free Wi-Fi throughout the inn, but don't look for a television. "We

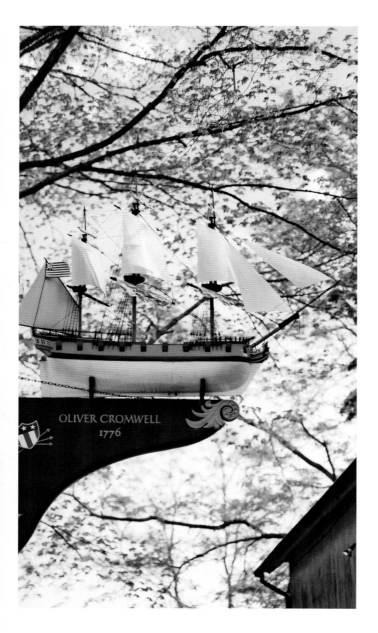

want people to experience the Tap Room," says Joan. "When they embrace it, they are glad that they didn't just sit in their room and blindly turn on CNN."

All rates include a simple, continental breakfast of muffins, coffee, toast, juice, and fruit, which will set you up for a day on the town. Essex is still a big boating and sailing community, so plan on heading out to the water during your visit. Fill the time between meals with an Essex Steam Train & Riverboat tour along the Connecticut River—it's the only remaining steam engine and riverboat connection in the country. Or walk down to the Town Wharf and enjoy a schooner cruise aboard the Mary E, a 75-foot wooden sloop at the Connecticut River Maritime Museum. During the one-and-a-half-hour sail you will hear tales of Essex's maritime history while keeping an eye out for wildlife. You also get free admission to the museum with the purchase of your ticket.

When you've had your fill, head back to The Gris to relax. The Paul family is passionate about its commitment to the Griswold Inn and Essex, and they will be sure to take care of you. Says Joan, "It is a very challenging business, but we all love being a part of it."

36 Main Street • Essex, CT 06426
(860) 767-1176 • griswoldinn.com

Ordinary

ESTABLISHED: 1638

A Modern Tavern with Historic Bona Fides

Located on the New Haven Green, Ordinary has taken over an abandoned, landmark space and has given an old bar the new life it deserves.

There's a mounted moose head over the fireplace that lends an air of casual ambiance, while a long ornately carved dark wood bar and high ornamental plastered ceilings add an air of grandeur. But it's not all about atmosphere—New Haven's Ordinary has some of the best drinks anywhere.

The bar's latest incarnation began in 2013 when a group of friends and restaurant industry pros headed by Jason Sobocinski (of Caseus Fromagerie & Bistro) and his brother Tom Sobocinski partnered with Mike Faber and Tim Cabral to take over the bar space of Richter's Café, a 30-year-old Yale bar famed for selling half yards of beer to the college crowd.

"Since the 1600s, there has always been some kind of establishment that offered food and drink on this corner of New Haven. The space itself has tons of history. It's pretty wild," says Cabral.

Sailors, students, and politicians were the tavern's early patrons. Situated not far from New Haven Harbor, in colonial times, the tavern was handy to the sailors debarking (disembark is better) from the sailing ships that docked at the city's piers. Yale moved from Old Saybrook to New Haven in 1716, and then, as now, students enjoyed malted beverages. And for more than a century, from 1701 to 1873, when New Haven was the joint capitol of Connecticut with Hartford, the tavern enjoyed a large political clientele.

The original building on this site was built in 1646 as a fine mansion, owned by Stephen Goodyear, one of New Haven's first settlers. A prominent landowner and active in town affairs, Goodyear eventually became deputy governor of the colony. Perhaps it is not so surprising, then, that Goodyear was given exclusive brewing privileges for the young colony.

In 1659 John Harriman resided at this address. He kept it as a tavern and the house took the name Ordinary, as places that also served food for the public were then called. When Cabral

explains the different meanings of the bar's name, he's most comfortable emphasizing the idea of ordinary in the context of the bar's diverse customers. "We are a local bar, a Yale bar, really we are an everyone bar."

By the mid-1700s, the building was known as Beer's Tavern. It was still one of the finest buildings in town when on June 28, 1775, future President George Washington, then commanding general of the Continental Army, slept here on his march from Philadelphia to Cambridge to end the Siege of Boston.

In 1850 the original tavern structure was demolished. In its place the New Haven Hotel was built. It was a grand enterprise for the time, a five-story stone and brick building with lodging for as many as 200 people. There was also a dining room that included the handsome bar that was eventually rescued and has become the architectural highlight of today's Ordinary.

At the turn of the 20th century, the New Haven Hotel was razed yet again to make way for the Taft Hotel. This elegant 12-story stone and brick building featured 450 rooms, a ballroom, and a basement pool. At the time, it was considered one of the best hotels in New England.

In its heyday during the first half of the 20th century, the Taft Hotel played host to countless dignitaries and celebrities. Its location next to the Shubert Theater and close to Yale attracted a steady stream of both academics and theater types. A short list includes Albert Einstein, Eleanor Roosevelt, Marlon Brando, and Richard Rogers and Oscar Hammerstein.

During Prohibition, the Taft Hotel's bar activity relocated deep into the bowels of the building. For a subterranean space, it was large with plenty of room to accommodate a big-band orchestra, a dance floor, and a glamorous cocktail-swilling crowd. In those days revelers could enter the bar surreptitiously through one of the underground tunnels that crisscrossed New Haven. After Prohibition, the bar was reopened upstairs and styled as an English Pub and named the Tap Room.

Before 1969, when Yale became coeducational, the Taft was considered "proper" lodging for the single young women visiting campus to attend the weekend mixers and football games. When it closed in 1973, the building steadily deteriorated until the 1980s when it was purchased and converted into the Taft Apartments. But some of the old hotel's design elements remained—including its soaring lobby rotunda and a stained glass ceiling. The Taft Tap room was shuttered.

Then, in 1983, the Tap Room was given a new beginning when Richter Elser, a then recent Yale graduate, rescued the bar instead of going to Harvard Law. Richter renovated the Tap Room space, including restoring the ornate woodwork surrounding the bar. Each panel features intricately carved flowers, leaves, and thorns. Together all the panels are said to reveal a numeric code, but several pieces of the bar are missing. It's been rumored that Yale's Skull & Bones Society keeps a panel at "The Tomb," the group's clubhouse. Cabral discloses that he and his partners have another panel that is also not up. Is this just another Bones conspiracy theory? It certainly is bestseller literary thriller material—and makes for a damn good story while sitting at the bar. The bar operated successfully until 2011, when it shut its doors until Cabral and his partners purchased it.

Cabral and his partners have tremendous reverence for the space. Honoring the legacy of Richter's is also important to these guys. While Ordinary's modern-day speakeasy beverage program and local artisanal menu are very different from Richter's beer bar vibe, much of Richter's memorabilia is intact. The magnificent moose head was shot by Elser's great grandfather in 1908 and is on long-term loan to the bar. The bar also has Richter's half-yard glasses on display, "Although we use them only at happy hour. We don't want people drinking half yards at the end of the night," laughs Cabral.

They certainly put a lot of technique into everything that they do at Ordinary. This is a cocktail-forward bar, but with a streamlined menu. There are only eight cocktails, but all are outstanding and each a little surprising. For the Sazerac, a chilled rye whiskey is mixed with simple syrup and bitters, then double strained with a twist of orange peel into a chilled absinthe-coated glass. What you won't find here? Soda guns or bottled mixers. Instead, they use craft bottles of soda and citrus they have juiced themselves. The partners are constantly rotating beers and wines on and off their small list—always looking for ways to test and expand their customers taste experiences.

Ordinary also manages to serve a mean bar menu from its miniscule kitchen. Imbibers can enjoy charcuterie and cheese boards, smoked-meat plates served with house pickles, and snacks such as candied bacon and beer cheese with pretzel bread. The grilled cheese sandwich is stellar—and it comes with a tomato soup dip.

Recapturing the old magic of a historic space heavy with nostalgia is a tall order. "Everyone here, including the partners and staff, are like-minded," says Cabral. "We share the same sense of quality of the product and quality of life inside and outside of our jobs that translates into everything we do. We have a lot of pride in everything we have here. We do what we do, and we try to do it in the most welcoming way we can. We are making new memories here."

990 Chapel Street • New Haven, CT 06510 • (203) 907-0238 • ordinarynewhaven.com

Winvian Farm

ESTABLISHED: 1775

Polished Rural Charm in the Litchfield Hills

Oak, hickory, and chestnut. These hard woods are water-resistant and have long been prized as material for the underwater portions of boats. 18th-century British naval might was made possible partly by American shipwrights. In colonial times, hard woods suitable for shipbuilding were among the riches of Connecticut's Litchfield Hills.

Located in the remote, northwest corner of the state, the Litchfield Hills feature the kind of quaint villages, idyllic farmscapes, and verdant rolling hills generally associated with Vermont.

In Morris, one of the smallest of these hill towns, through the gate of a nearly hidden enclave, sits Winvian, an upscale resort of 18 themed cabins set among wooded groves. The main building, a pretty three-story, white clapboard house, is surrounded by acres of vegetable gardens along with a two-story red barn in the back. The overall setting is as much working estate as it is New England country inn.

The main house, the inn's most historic structure, was built as a private residence for prominent local physician, Dr. Seth Bird, in 1775. With its central chimney, creaky floorboards, and rough-hewn beams, it is a wonderful example of early Federal architecture. And in typical Yankee fashion, the house was built with miscellaneous, sometimes scavenged, materials.

Maggie Smith, the resort's developer and owner, describes how in the course of renovating the property in 2003, her chief engineer found thick chestnut planking hiding in the interior walls of the farmhouse and buried out in the woods. "He told me that chestnut boards were valuable, and it wasn't uncommon for the colonists to hide them from the British who would either commandeer them or tax them. We reused them all in the restoration."

From the time of Dr. Bird's death, the property seems to have passed from one Litchfield Hills farming family to another. "My kids' paternal grandparents, Winthrop and Vivian Smith, bought this property in 1948. The property is surrounded by 4,000-plus acres of the White Memorial

Foundation Preserve. They realized back then that there was a value in being buffered. I still think it was brilliant of them," says Maggie.

"Win" and Vivian Smith lived in New York City, where Win was a founding partner of Merrill Lynch, Pierce, Fenner & Smith, as the brokerage house was once known. The couple combined Win and Vivian to name their country retreat Win-Vian, where they spent weekends enjoying time with their family—which now included their son, Win Junior.

Win Senior died in 1961, and Vivian continued to live at Winvian for many decades before passing away in 1998. Maggie recalls how her four kids grew up visiting Grandma Vivian at the farm.

Maggie runs the resort with the help of her oldest daughter Heather as Managing Director and her son Win Smith III as Director of Sales and Marketing.

"My goal in developing the property was to preserve the farm and honor the Smith legacy. This seemed to be the best way to do it. I am pleased we are keeping it in the family."

Winvian is the definition of rustic chic. The resort is both fun and whimsical while offering the highest-end luxury—from its exceedingly well-appointed cottages, to its world-class restaurant with a top-echelon chef, to its pampering spa, along with an abundance of activity options including an outdoor pool, bicycles (each cottage comes with two), and yoga classes.

If you crave wide-plank floors, a wood-burning fireplace, and period antiques, then Winvian's Hadley Suite is for you. The suite takes over the entire upper floor of the Seth Byrd House and has its own private entrance. An elegant and timeless blue and white toile pattern is used for wallcoverings, furniture, and bedding. The king-size, four-poster bed is decked out in fine linens and is perfectly positioned to capture the views of the front lawn and the open fields beyond.

The Hadley Suite's adjoining fireplaced living room and office nook take inspiration from chinoiserie, which was quite the fashion in wealthier colonial homes. The room is a colorful mélange of crimson wallpaper, vintage black lacquer accent tables, Chinese porcelains, and an ivory slipcovered sofa bed.

The Hadley Suite's bathroom is sumptuous with marble flooring, dual sinks, a whirlpool tub, and a steam shower. And those Bulgari bath products are a nice touch.

If you prefer to retire to more fanciful lodgings, you'll find each of the 18 designed cottages has a unique personality. With names like "Stable," "Artist," and "Golf" and inspired decor to match, there is certainly something for every taste. Beaver, for instance, features a chandelier made of driftwood, a river stone fireplace, and a bed frame made of tree trunks over which an actual beaver dam

is reworked as an art piece. All the bathrooms are wonderful, with rain showerheads and spa tubs. Each cottage also has a private entrance. All rates include a bountiful breakfast with freshly made pastries and a choice of several entrees.

The informal grandeur of the resort's main lobby is as impressive as the design of the cottages with a cathedral ceiling, floor-to-ceiling windows, and giant stone fireplaces. There is a billiard table, board games, jigsaw puzzles, and several cozy seating areas.

In the evening, guests often congregate around the fire pit on the lobby patio, and s'mores are a regular occurrence.

Winvian's restaurant is a destination in its own right and is open to the public. The kitchen is helmed by Executive Chef Chris Eddy. "Chef has been with us since we opened. I am very lucky to have him," says Maggie.

Trained in the kitchens of Daniel Boulud and Alain Ducasse, Eddy specializes in innovative American cuisine with a European flair. His menus celebrate the season and what is available from Winvian Farm that day—and therefore are always changing.

Eddy tantalizes diners with dishes such as lamb ragout with pecorino and Meyer lemon or Winvian pork with foraged ramps, rhubarb, and currants. Chef Eddy supervises three-and-a-half acres of vegetables, fruits, and herbs from Winvian's gardens and orchard. He also taps almost exclusively local suppliers for everything else. Says Maggie, "Guests love that Chef chooses a menu using ingredients from the garden."

Dinners at Winvian are elaborate, candle-lit affairs. And while the food is exceptional, what puts the dining experience truly over the top is the service. The dining room manager Stefano Middei is part savant and part psychic—he knows every wine in Winvian's extensive cellar and is so attuned to his guests that they rarely have to flag him.

And if you prefer to dine in front of the fire in the homestead's original 18th-century dining room, simply ask. It's an enchanting space and true to the period with copper pots and kettles that hang over the hearth, a mix of antiques, white linens, and candlelight.

Asked about her typical customers, Maggie says that they are often repeat visitors. "If we can get them here, chances are they will come back. We've just had a guest on a 35th stay."

155 Alain White Road • Morris, CT 06763
(860) 567-9600 • winvian.com

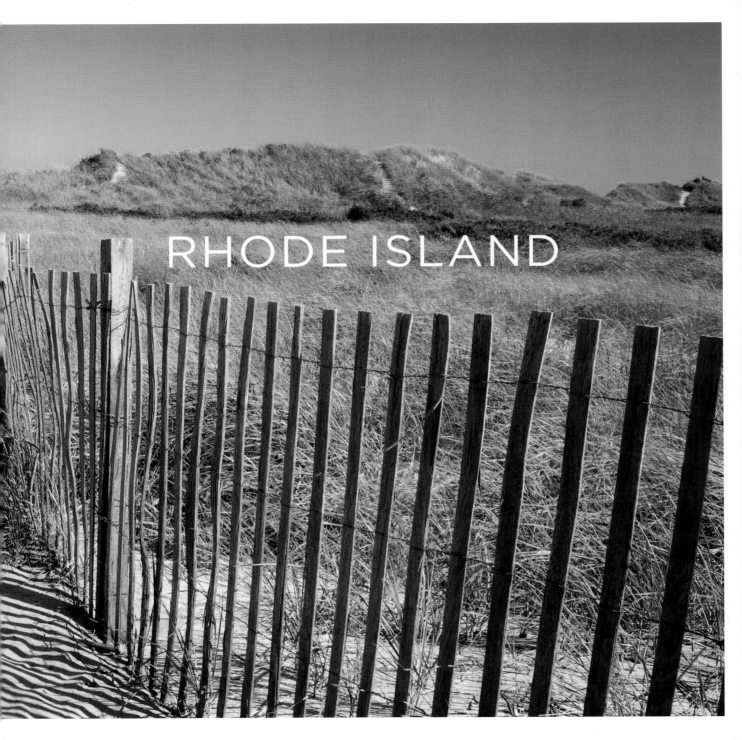

RHODE ISLAND

Frances Malbone House

CIRCA: 1760

Centuries Later, Still Welcoming Romance

Some people think that bed-and-breakfasts exist only in the countryside. Behind a butter-cream yellow façade, this 20-room townhouse inn in the midst of Newport proves otherwise. And even though the hotel is located in the liveliest part of town—just steps away from Newport Harbor—the overall feel of the inn is of serenity and quiet.

Take a stroll along narrow Thames Street today and it is not difficult to imagine bustling colonial Newport with the sea on one side and its concentration of distinguished merchants' homes with commanding views of Narragansett Bay on the other.

During the pre–Revolutionary War period, Newport welcomed religious minorities, including a large number of Quakers and Jewish immigrants—and both groups were instrumental in making Newport the colonies' leading slave port in the mid-1700s. At the time Newport boasted more than 20 distilleries that shipped and sold rum for African slaves who were then traded to the West Indies for more molasses and sugar to be boiled into yet more rum.

Francis Malbone was one of Newport's most prosperous shipping merchants and a slave trader when he bought the waterfront Thames Street property in 1758. Two years later he had the handsome Colonial Georgian mansion built for his family. Designed by Peter Harrison, one of the colonies' most accomplished architects (he also designed Boston's King's Chapel and Newport's Redwood Library), the house is considered an excellent example of colonial residential architecture. The three-story dwelling embodies 18th-century ornamentation with its elegant proportions, pedimented doorways, and finely crafted interior finishes.

As befitting their role in society, the Malbones were patrons of the arts. There is a portrait of Frances Malbone's sons, Francis Jr. and Saunders, by noted colonial portraitist Gilbert Stuart in the inn's front hallway. It's a copy of the original, which hangs in Boston's Museum of Fine Arts, but it still welcomes visitors to the Malbone family home.

The Francis Malbone House also has a legacy of intrigue. Malbone was not only a shrewd businessman, but he had Federalist sympathies. He had a tunnel built from the basement of his house to his wharf to hide goods and avoid paying custom duties to the King. He was promptly shut down, however, by the British who governed Newport at the time.

But despite the British occupation of the city, or because of it, the Malbone House was the setting of a wartime romance. The story goes that Francis Malbone's daughter Peggy fell in love with a young British officer. After the war, the forbidden sweethearts married and returned to England, where he became Lord Stanhope, Earl of Chesterfield, and together they lived out the remainder of their days.

The Malbone family sold the house in the early 1800s, and it passed through a series of owners. In the 1960s the mansion was restored to its original colonial design. It was still a private home when, in 1989, current owner Will Dewey, having just graduated from Johnson & Wales, along with some partners, bought the building and transformed it into an inn.

Says Will, "For the first six years we had nine guest bedrooms. We didn't have enough rooms. We were always full. It was a nice problem to have. We looked around to purchase another property in town and there wasn't anything with this caliber of historic significance and parking, but we had this land in the back that was like a park. So we hired an architect and designed a courtyard wing addition. We pretty much doubled the size of the house. We went from nine rooms to eighteen. And then in 2000 we purchased a cottage in the back and added two suites."

Will still fluffs the throw pillows in the front parlor every morning and neatly stacks the newspapers. "I want there to be a wow factor when the guests arrive," he says. Will has lived and breathed the Francis Malbone House for more than 25 years. So why does he do it? "I got into this business because all my hobbies and my career are rolled into one. I like to cook. I like to garden. I like real estate. I love people. I'm a people person. I like to go to work every day because I don't feel that it is work."

Inside, the entire first floor is dedicated to common areas, including two parlors, a library, and a dining room. The rooms have an overall romantic, 19th-century ambiance that features working fireplaces, oversized tufted couches, finely upholstered wing back chairs, and an eclectic mix of antiques and artwork. But the inn's homey touches—the gourmet breakfasts, the afternoon tea with homemade treats, fresh flowers in every room, and a library honor bar, are what transport you back centuries.

Outside follow the sound of the trickling fountain to the inn's lush courtyard, where the air is perfumed with the scent of flowers and crepe myrtle. Here, there is both shade and sun for enjoying a morning cup of coffee or a pre-dinner drink.

As for the guest rooms, all are gracious, featuring carved mahogany canopy and four-poster beds and comforters that call to mind venerable European hotels.

Will and his staffers have that knack for remembering guests' names when they come back for another visit, which they do often. Repeat visitors make up 60 percent of the inn's bookings. Will says that people come back to the Francis Malbone House because of the personal service. "We can help them plan their entire day—whether it's visiting the mansions or strolling the Cliff Walk. We want them to have a good time, we want them to enjoy the house, and we want them to come back to Newport."

392 Thames Street • Newport, RI 02840 • (800) 846-0392 • malbone.com

Mount Hope Farm

ESTABLISHED: 1680

A Settlement Era Property and Colonial Estate

Located between Providence and Newport, Bristol is a quaint New England town with three centuries of seafaring heritage. Perched at the tip of a peninsula between Narragansett and Mount Hope Bays, Bristol boasts postcard-perfect water views, trendy gastro pubs, and beautiful stretches of sandy beach. It's a patriotic town too—known for having the country's oldest Fourth of July parade.

Just five minutes away from Bristol Harbor lies Mount Hope Farm, a sprawling estate of 127 acres and 6 historic buildings that include the Governor Bradford House Inn. What is most striking about this landscape is that in its more than 400 years, Mount Hope Farm has spanned a broad sweep of Rhode Island history.

The original Mount Hope Lands grant was part of Plimoth Colony and was established in 1680 by Nathaniel Byfield, a wealthy Boston merchant. Eventually, Byfield's granddaughter, Elizabeth Macintosh Royall, inherited the property. Elizabeth was married to Isaac Royall II of Massachusetts, one of the founders of Harvard Law School and a member of one of the largest slave-holding families in New England.

Isaac built the original two-and-a-half-story Georgian home in 1745. The interior was lavish for the time and designed to impress with rooms of excellent proportions that included many examples of hand-carved woodwork.

In the 1780s William Bradford acquired the house. "The house is named for Bradford," explains innkeeper David Rubino. "He was deputy governor of Rhode Island in the late 1700s. He was a war hero, a doctor, and a lawyer. He was a little bit of everything. He was a very prominent member of this community. The British burned down a lot of downtown Bristol. We were set away from downtown, and because we were owned by a Loyalist, this home was spared."

The house passed through many different hands, receiving various updates, including two-story additions in 1840 and 1890, until Rudolph Haffenreffer II bought it in 1917. He was an entrepreneur, and most notably a brewery magnate and head of Rhode Island–based Narragansett

Brewery. Executive director of the farm Jennifer Bristol says Haffenreffer was "a real entertainer. He loved to have parties." Haffenreffer was also a philanthropist. "This amazing person was a conservationist. He was thinking much bigger picture than people of that time were. That is what we are preserving," says Jennifer.

The Haffenreffer family owned the home and used it as their summer residence for more than 80 years before it was purchased by the nonprofit Mount Hope Trust. The trust acts as a steward for the farm and manages access to the Brown University–owned holdings, which include King Philip's seat and the Haffenreffer Museum of Anthropology, which houses one of the largest Native American collections in the country.

"We have a lot to offer," says David. "The historic part of this farm is huge. This was the home of the Wampanoag tribe. This is where Massasoit, one of the most iconic Indians, lived. To think what this property, with its old-growth forest, looked like 300 to 400 years ago. It's amazing."

Indeed, the history is astonishing. The ancestors of today's Wampanoag settled these lands for millennia. According to Jennifer, "Mount Hope was a key piece of land and the colonists wanted it. They knew they could grow here, because the Indians were and they were going to get it."

A big part of Jennifer's job is to work with the Wampanoag tribe to tell their story and make it accessible. "I think it is a place that needs to be seen to be appreciated," she says. "My job is to make sure everyone knows it's here. My job is also to make sure that no one knows it's here. The human footprint can be disastrous at times."

The Pokanoket Indians were the dominant tribe of the Wampanoag Nation. Their territory encompassed much of southern New England, including large areas of Massachusetts, Connecticut, and Rhode Island. The Pokanoket sachem, or leader, during the early 17th century was Massasoit. In the fall of 1621, Massasoit brought 90 Wampanoag to Plimoth for a traditional harvest feast, which would later be known as the First Thanksgiving. But Massasoit's true legacy was that he was first sachem to sign a peace treaty with the Plimoth colonists—an alliance that lasted nearly 50 years.

The Wampanoag's tribal seat was in the shadow of Mount Hope (Montaup in the Pokanoket language) along the eastern shore of Narragansett Bay. Says Jennifer Bristol, "This area, this entire landscape, was the summer hunting and fishing grounds for the Wampanoag tribe. They would have arrived here in mid-May and stayed until mid- to late November. It had access to the bay, forested areas, and fresh water with streams."

When Massasoit died in 1661, his son Metacom became the leader of the Wampanoag. Nicknamed King Philip, "he was a bit of a dandy," says Jennifer. In 1676 he led the Wampanoag uprising

against the colonists. What would become known as "King Philip's War" was among the most deadly and bloodiest wars in American history.

"On the night King Philip died, there was a lot of death in this forest," says Jennifer. King Philip's seat is the rocky outcropping at the base of Mount Hope, where King Philip slept on the last night of his life with his tribe around him: men, women, children, and elders. The colonists attacked and King Philip escaped over the mountain, right into an ambush on the other side. King Philip was shot by a man named John Alderman, a former member of the Wampanoag who had become Christian, what was known as a "praying Indian." They quartered and dismembered King Philip, giving his hand to Alderman and putting his head on a spike at Plimoth Plantation, where it remained for some 20 years.

King Philip's seat is still sacred ground. "When the tribe comes here now, there is a real sense of loss," says Jennifer. The descendants of the Pokanokets number in the hundreds, and spiritual gatherings for the tribe—praying, drumming circles, and the summer solstice ceremony where arrows are shot into the sky to tie the sun to the ground for the harvest—still take place here.

Mount Hope Farm is many things to many people. A stay here can truly transport you back in time. Over the years the entire structure has been sensibly altered for modern living, but the bones of the main house have largely remained historic and accurate. All together there are 12 rooms on the property for guests, each with its own character. The Haffenreffer Room is the grandest of them all with pale yellow walls and antique pieces (including a lovely writing desk) offset by timeworn hardwood floors. The pin-neat main inn offers four rooms, while the rest are in two separate houses on the property.

Guests can start their day with a hearty breakfast of scrambled or fried eggs (laid from the farm's chickens) served alongside entrees such David's cream cheese–stuffed french toast with berries. Then head out to explore the farm and the adjacent 375-acre reserve owned by Brown University. A network of walking trails takes visitors through the farm, around the vegetable or old-fashioned rose gardens, down to the ponds, or out to the 1919 Adirondack-style cabin where they can watch the last of the sunset on the shore of Mount Hope Bay.

"It is a big debate among my board. One will say that Mount Hope should be a retreat, another person says we should do events, somebody else says we should be a full working farm, and someone else says we should be a historic site," says Jennifer. "I say, yes, Mount Hope Farm has to be all of those things."

---

250 Metacom Avenue • Bristol, RI 02809 • (401) 254-1745 • mounthopefarm.org

White Horse Tavern

ESTABLISHED: 1673

From Serving Grog to Pirates to Presiding as One of Newport's Finest Restaurants

Before Newport was known as the playground of the Vanderbilts and Astors, the city was one of North America's principal ports, exporting fish, whale oil, and lumber during colonial times. By 1750 Newport was also the colony's major slave market—trading rum for slaves and molasses. At the time, the city rivaled Boston and New York as a trade and cultural center.

In those days colonial Newport was also rife with pirates, privateers, and smugglers—unsavory characters all—in a time of great civil unrest.

In its early years, the White Horse Tavern served as the meeting place for the Colony of Rhode Island and Providence Plantation's General Assembly, its Criminal Court, and the Newport City Council. As colonial grievances against the British spread, many took to the tavern to argue and debate what needed to be done. Countless tankards were raised and drained at the White Horse Tavern. Newport myth says that Benjamin Franklin drank here on his frequent visits to his brother James's printing press in town.

Today the White Horse Tavern takes great pride in its history of scalawaggery, as well it should. It is one of the oldest taverns in the country. Like many colonial-era taverns, the White Horse Tavern began life as a private home. The two-story, two-room building was constructed at the corner of Marlborough and Farwell, then a lightly traveled street, two blocks from Newport's wharves for Francis Brinley. The house was then acquired by William Mayes, enlarged in 1673, and converted into a tavern.

Keeper Jonathan Nichols named it the White Horse Tavern in 1730. In the days when not everyone could read, it was common for the symbolism of tavern signs to indicate the loyalties of the tavern owner. Since the colonists were essentially English, ties to Britain were still strong; trade and shop signs often used elements of aristocratic heraldry. A white horse was the badge of the House of

Hanover, the ruling British dynasty of the time. During the 1776 British occupation of Newport, the British took over the tavern and used it to billet its Hessian mercenaries. By then, the Nichols family's sympathies were no longer Loyalist. Proprietor Walter Nichols (Jonathan's son) moved to New York until after the war. When he returned in 1780, he enlarged the tavern to its present size.

The tavern stayed in the Nichols family for nearly 200 years. In 1895 the property became a boarding house. By the 1950s, Newport experienced a prolonged period of urban decay and the tavern was neglected. It was dilapidated until the Preservation Society of Newport interceded to save it.

The White Horse Tavern's dark red clapboard siding, gambrel roof, and pedimented doorway contribute to its architectural distinction. It is considered by many to be one of the finest examples of colonial architecture in Newport.

The White Horse Tavern is both welcoming and welcomed by locals and tourists alike. Inside there's a general New England quaintness to the space, with its wide plank floors, exposed beams, candle-lit white-clothed tables, and American Windsor spindle chairs. In the cool weather months, the warmth of the fireplaces can be felt throughout the intimate dining rooms. The wait staff is young and cheerful, the service attentive, and the wine list smartly priced. Dining here is posh, but unfussy. The team behind the White Horse Tavern today is owner Jeff Farrar and executive chef Rich Silvia.

Together they offer a menu that embraces the Rhode Island food scene and is built on a strong relationship with local purveyors. Chef Silvia knows what he's doing with the bounty from the deep. The Rhode Island clam chowder, clear-broth soup of tender clams, is enhanced with fresh thyme. Dishes are refined yet gutsy, such as the heritage pork tenderloin with native sweet corn succotash and cocoa nibs, or the black garlic and lemon pan-roasted chicken. Silvia's showstopper dishes are his riffs on two Continental classics. His butter-poached lobster is a generous serving of lobster meat accompanied by roasted carrots, fingerlings, and a lobster tarragon emulsion. The beef Wellington is worth ordering for its foie gras pâté alone, never mind the expertly cooked beef tenderloin and luxurious Madeira sauce.

The tavern offers a much more relaxed environment at lunch, featuring crowd pleasers such as rustic salads, hearty sandwiches, and Silvia's signature fried duck Scotch egg wrapped in sausage.

A dark and stormy cocktail—dark rum and ginger beer garnished with lime—should begin your meal. The drink is a traditional sailor's cocktail up and down the entire east coast, and the bar at the White Horse Tavern makes a great one.

A step into the White Horse Tavern whisks diners back more than two centuries to the earliest days of America's founding. Chef Silvia's inspired re-creations of regional New England favorites, along with the tavern's overall feeling of warmth and hospitality, invite guests to linger, making the White Horse Tavern one of the most enjoyable colonial dining experiences in New England.

---

26 Marlborough Street • Newport, RI 02840 • (401) 849-3600 • whitehorsenewport.com

TAVERN MUSEUMS

If you can't get enough of visiting still-operating colonial era watering holes and inns, there are dozens of colonial era tavern museums scattered throughout the region for you to tour.

Major historical sites such as the Minuteman National Historic site and Portsmouth's Strawberry Banke, small town historical societies, state governments, and various hereditary societies (such as the Daughters of the American Revolution) have preserved many of New England's network of Revolutionary War taverns and inns as historic house museums.

You can't imbibe at any of these places, but each offers insight into the role of the earliest days of American drinking and dining. Be sure to check, too, for special seasonal events.

Many of these tavern museums are small and are staffed by volunteers, so their open hours can be extremely limited. A lot of these sites are only open seasonally, so be sure to call in advance to confirm days and hours when planning a visit. Many are happy to accommodate visits by appointment with advance notice.

Buckman Tavern

CIRCA: 1710

1 Bedford Street • Lexington, MA 02420 • (781) 862-5598 • lexingtonhistory.org
Open March through November

In the wee hours of the morning of April 19, 1775, Captain Parker and his colonial militiamen fortified themselves with liquid courage for the fight against the British at Buckman Tavern before marching out onto Lexington Green and into the history books.

Golden Ball Tavern Museum

CIRCA: 1768

662 Boston Post Road • Weston, MA 02493 • (781) 894-1751 • goldenballtavern.org
Open by appointment

At the time of the Revolution, this two-story, Georgian-style home in the center of Weston, Massachusetts, was a popular tavern located just 17 miles outside of Boston. Isaac Jones, a prominent publican, owned the tavern. When visited by two Boston travelers (spies of General Gage), Jones welcomed them with open arms—and served them tea—so they knew they were in the company of a like-minded Tory.

Hall Tavern

CIRCA: 1760

Historic Deerfield • 80 Old Main Street • Deerfield, MA 01342 • historic-deerfield.org
Open year-round, check website for days and hours

"The Street" is Historic Deerfield's quaint thoroughfare lined with 18th- and 19th-century homes (many open to the public). Some buildings were moved to Deerfield from other New England towns. Hall Tavern dates from 1760 and was originally located in nearby Charlmont. Hall Tavern (appropriately) serves as the museum's main visitor center and should be your first stop upon arrival. The museum's popular open-hearth cooking demonstrations take place here.

Harnden Tavern

CIRCA: 1770

Wilmington Town Museum • 430 Salem Street • Wilmington, MA 01887 • (978) 658-5475 • wilmingtonma.gov
Open year-round, check website for days and times

This tavern is named after Colonel Joshua Harnden, a Revolutionary War veteran who returned to his hometown of Wilmington (then a rural village) to open an inn. There is evidence that in the years prior to the Civil War the home was a stop on the Underground Railroad helping runaway slaves from the South reach Canada. Visitors can see the presumed hiding place next to the fireplace.

Hartwell Tavern

CIRCA: 1732

Minute Man National Historic Park • 136 North Great Road • Lincoln, MA 017738 • (781) 674-1920
nps.gov/mima/index.htm • Open Memorial Day through October

During the Revolutionary War era, the home of Ephraim and Elizabeth Hartwell was also a tavern. The farmhouse was located on the road trod by British soldiers on April 19, 1775, from Lexington to Concord and on their retreat back to Boston. Ranger-led musket drill demonstrations take place outside the tavern throughout the day—cover your ears!

Munroe Tavern

CIRCA: 1735

1332 Massachusetts Avenue • Lexington, MA 02420 • (781) 862-0295 • lexingtonhistory.org
Open April through October

During the Battle of Lexington and Concord on April 19, 1775, Munroe Tavern was briefly commandeered by the British Army as their field hospital and command post as they retreated to Boston. Shortly after taking office in 1789, George Washington visited the hallowed ground of Lexington Green and dined at Munroe Tavern during his tour of New England.

The Old Ordinary

CIRCA: 1668

Hingham Historical Society • 21 Lincoln Street • Hingham, MA 02043 • (781) 749-7721 • hinghamhistorical.org
Open mid-June through Labor Day, Tuesday through Sunday; by appointment the rest of the year

This house was built by Thomas Andrews, one of the founding fathers of Hingham, in 1668 and was a stopping place on the Boston to Plymouth road for more than 150 years. Originally a two-room dwelling, the house was enlarged in the 1740s and the 1760s to better accommodate travelers on the popular thoroughfare. Today the building is the headquarters of the Hingham Historical Society. The 14 rooms include a taproom, kitchen, formal parlor, and tool room, and all are furnished with historic artifacts in the style of the 18th century. Be sure to explore the tavern's beautifully designed gardens.

Parker Tavern

CIRCA: 1694

103 Washington Street • Reading, MA 01867 • No phone • friendsofparkertavern.org
Open Sundays, May through October

Fifteen miles north of Boston, this 17th-century, two-story saltbox colonial was built as a private home for Abraham Bryant, a farmer and blacksmith. During the late 1700s, Ephraim Parker acquired the property and operated part of his home as a licensed tavern. Its original structure remains largely intact, and today the museum houses artifacts documenting Reading's historic ties to the Revolutionary War.

Rider's Tavern

Established: 1799

255 Stafford Street • Charlton, MA 01507 • (508) 248-7113 • charltonhistoricalsociety.org
Open by appointment

Twelve miles west of Worcester, the building of this fine twenty-one-room Federal period tavern in Charlton was begun by local innkeeper Eli Wheelock in 1797. Sadly, Wheelock died before its completion and brothers Isaiah and William Rider completed the building. With its taproom, public dining room, separate ladies parlor, and second-floor ballroom, Rider's Tavern is an excellent example of colonial-era hostelry and was one of the nicer taverns along the Worcester to Hartford stagecoach run.

Burnham Tavern

CIRCA: 1770

14 Colonial Way • Machias, ME 04654 • (207) 733-4577 • burnhamtavern.com
Open July through September

In June 1775, just months after the Battles of Lexington and Concord, this secluded hamlet on the rocky coast of Maine was the sight of one of the first naval battles of the Revolutionary War. Burnham Tavern was the gathering place for Jeremiah O'Brien and his scrappy band of Machias men, who forced the surrender of the HMS Margaretta, a British ship on its way to Boston loaded with Maine lumber.

Jefferds Tavern

CIRCA: 1750

Museums of Old York • 3 Lindsay Road • York, ME • (207) 363-1756 • oldyork.org
Open all year, days and hours vary seasonally

Originally situated on the King's Highway in Wells, this 1750 colonial tavern was a popular stopover for horsemen riding the road from Portsmouth to Portland. The tavern was dismantled and moved to York in the early 1940s and was fully restored. Inside the dark-reddish-brown structure, the wood-paneled tavern presents a picture of 18th-century tavern life, complete with a cage bar, a cooking hearth, and a beehive brick oven (which today is used for cooking demonstrations).

Keeler Tavern Museum

CIRCA: 1713

132 Main Street • Ridgefield, CT 06877 • (203) 438-5485 • keelertavernmuseum.org
Open March through December

Dating back to 1709, Ridgefield is one of Connecticut's oldest towns. Located on the Boston Post Road but originally built as a family home for Benjamin Hoyt, the Keeler Tavern was turned into an inn and tavern by his grandson Timothy Keeler in 1772. Guides in colonial dress recount the Battle of Ridgefield, the 1777 skirmish between colonial troops led by Benedict Arnold and British troops. A token of the battle—a British cannonball lodged in one of the tavern's corner posts—is a tour highlight.

Phelps Tavern Museum

Phelps Tavern Museum

CIRCA: 1771

800 Hopemeadow Street • Simsbury, CT 06070 • (860) 658-2500 • simsburyhistory.org

Property of the Simsbury Historic Society, this Georgian-style residence located just north of Hartford was part of the Phelps family homestead. Established by the family patriarch Noah Phelps, a Revolutionary War hero, the house was operated as a tavern from 1786 until 1849 by three generations of the Phelps family. The permanent exhibits provide a glimpse of daily life and tavern keeping in New England during the 18th and early 19th centuries. The complex includes a meetinghouse, a barn, and a one-room schoolhouse.

Historic Putnam Cottage

CIRCA: 1690

243 East Putnam Avenue • Greenwich, CT 06830 • (203) 869-9697 • putnamcottage.org
By appointment

Located near the New York state border, Greenwich was attacked by pillaging British soldiers on February 26, 1779. General Israel Putnam escaped Greenwich by horseback to warn Stamford of the British advance. During the Revolutionary War years, this tavern was owned by the Knapp family. Today it is maintained by the Putnam Hill chapter of the Daughters of the American Revolution and focuses on Connecticut's role in the Revolutionary War.

Chimney Point Tavern

CIRCA: 1785

8149 VT Route 17 W • Addison, VT 05491 • (802) 759-2412 • historicsites.vermont.gov
Open May through October, check website for days and times

Chimney Point on the shores of Lake Champlain is one of Vermont's earliest and most strategic settlements. In early colonial times the territory's story was largely of tensions among the Native Americans, the French, and the English that culminated in Ethan Allen's capture of Fort Ticonderoga, just 12 miles away, on May 9, 1775. The original wood frame tavern, along with a ferry service, was built soon after the Revolutionary War. The tavern was substantially enlarged, becoming a resort in the early 1900s, but closing in 1934 after the opening of the Lake Champlain Bridge.

Old Constitution House

CIRCA: Mid 1700s

16 North Main Street • Windsor, VT • (802) 672-3773 • historicsites.vermont.gov
Open May through October, check website for days and times

Located along the Upper Valley of the Connecticut River and along the Vermont and New Hampshire border, the town of Windsor takes pride in its moniker of "birthplace of Vermont." It is also the home of a tavern once belonging to Elija West, now known as the Old Constitution House. Several period rooms in this tavern tell the story of 18th-century tavern keeping, but it's the table that's the real story. Believed to be from July 8, 1777, it was here that a group of delegates met to discuss, argue, debate, and ultimately vote on Vermont's Constitution.

Jones House & Tavern

CIRCA: 1700s

New Hampshire Farm Museum • 1305 White Mountain Highway
Milton, New Hampshire 03851
(603) 652-7840 • farmmuseum.org

Open June through Labor Day, Wednesday through Sunday,
check website for other opening times

From the 1700s, seven generations of Plummers and Joneses prospered on this land. The original farmhouse was a small house built by Joseph Plummer. In the early 1800s, Joseph's daughter Betsy married Levi Jones, and saw an opportunity to profit. The house was located at the halfway point of the stagecoach route between Conway and Boston. Jones expanded the house and ran a tavern and stagecoach stop for 50 years. The museum is a working, educational farm, giving visitors a peek into New Hampshire's rich farming heritage.

Folsom Tavern

CIRCA: 1775

American Independence Museum • 164 Water Street • Exeter, NH • (603) 772-2622
independencemuseum.org/share/folsom-tavern
Open May through November, Tuesday through Saturday

This colonial tavern has had many lives—as a railway waiting station, shoe repair shop, Chinese laundry, and dress store. Now a part of the American Independence Museum campus, this building exudes a sense of history. Guests can marvel at the ancient, wide pine floors and the simple rooms of this colonial-era tavern, where President Washington was the guest of honor when he visited during his 1789 New England tour. Among its prized possessions is a rare Dunlap broadside copy of the Declaration of Independence.

Pitt Tavern

Established: 1768

Strawberry Banke Museum • 14 Hancock Street • Portsmouth, NH 03801 • (603) 433-1100 • strawberrybanke.org
Open daily, check for times

Strawberry Banke, a waterfront neighborhood of Portsmouth, is nearly 400 years old. By the mid-1700s, the city was an established, prosperous coastal town. Local folk and travelers alike met at the William Pitt Tavern, including a number of notables such as John Hancock, the Marquise de Lafayette, and George Washington. Today, Pitt Tavern is part of the Strawberry Banke Museum, a living history museum of some 30 buildings that together tell the life of this neighborhood from the 1600s to the 1900s.

Wyman Tavern

CIRCA: 1762

339 Main Street • Keene, NH 03431 • (603) 352-1895 • hsccnh.org
Open June through Labor Day, Thursday through Saturday; May through mid-November by appointment

Located in New Hampshire's' Monadnock region, this 18th-century tavern has lots of history and lots of stories. On April 22, 1775, proprietor and captain of the local militia Isaac Wyman mustered a group of Keene volunteer soldiers to march toward Lexington to help the colonists in their fight with the British. Also, on October 22, 1770, the tavern was the site of the first meeting of the Trustees of Dartmouth College.

The Paine House Museum

CIRCA: 1691

7 Station Street • Coventry, RI 02816 • (401) 249-0633 • westernrihistory.org
Open Saturday, May through September

One of Rhode Island's oldest homes, this two-and-a-half-story, wood-frame building was known as Brayton Tavern during colonial times and was well located on the main road between Providence and Plainfield, Connecticut. The ground-level tavern has been restored and re-created to tell the story of colonial life in Western Rhode Island.

Photo Credits

Acknowledgments

New England's Colonial Inn's & Taverns could not have become a reality without the help of many others.

A huge thank you to each of the owners, managers and employees of the inns and taverns that I profiled for their enthusiasm for the project. I greatly appreciate the time you spent time not only participating in interviews but also often giving me a tour of your property.

I would like to thank my editor at Globe Pequot, Amy Lyons, who first proposed the idea of this book to me over a dinner of pasta and wine at a restaurant in Boston's Charlestown neighborhood.

Bill DeSousa -Mauk is a fantastic source for everything tourism- related on Cape Cod and the islands. He is also able to secure ferry tickets to Martha's Vineyard and Nantucket on short notice!

I am appreciative to my friends Amy Segal and Gail Herman for walking and listening.

I would like to thank my parents, Robert and Josephine Dascanio, for great travel genes. Both are in their late 70's and they still travel!

To my husband, Masoud Olia, thank you for giving me the space and time to pursue my writing career. For this book in particular, I'm grateful for your driving throughout the six-state region and your master skills of packing the car.

As always, many thanks go to my four children. Despite living in Los Angeles, my son Bijan can always be counted on for his enthusiasm for every one of my books. Thanks to my son Kian for watching over the house during my many weekends away and welcoming me when I came home. And special thanks to my son Camy who shares my love of history and patiently listens to my (long) stories of old New England.

Lastly, thank you to my daughter Leda for accompanying me on more than a few field trips and taking many of the photos in this book. Because who better than a college girl to take "Insta-gram" worthy pictures? I can't wait to see your own book dreams come true!

About the Author

Travel writer and essayist Maria Olia came to Boston to attend Northeastern University more than 35 years ago—and still loves the city just as much now as she did back then.

Maria's work has appeared in the *Boston Globe*, the *Christian Science Monitor*, and *Working Mother*. She has also written Globe Pequot's *Day Trips New England*, *Insiders' Guide to Massachusetts* and *Discovering Vintage Boston*.

As a result of reviewing and writing about so many restaurants, Maria has a passion for good food and wine. She also loves to share her cooking and baking with her adult children at Sunday dinner. And to compensate for her foodie tendencies, Maria is an avid walker.

When she is not writing, Maria can be found exploring Boston and Cambridge. Besides New England, her favorite travel destination is Italy. She lives with her husband in Newton, just outside of Boston.